Living with Computers

James W. Cortada

Living with Computers

The Digital World of Today and Tomorrow

 Springer

Copernicus Books is a brand of Springer

James W. Cortada
Charles Babbage Institute
University of Minnesota
Minneapolis, MN, USA

ISBN 978-3-030-34361-3   ISBN 978-3-030-34362-0   (eBook)
https://doi.org/10.1007/978-3-030-34362-0

This Copernicus imprint is published by the registered company Springer Nature Switzerland AG
The registered company address is: Gewerbestrasse 11, 6330 Cham, Switzerland

Preface

For well over half the human race, it has become nearly impossible to go through a full day without encountering computers. Most other humans, too, are subject to the same reality, just that they might not realize it. Three-fourths of the world is now connected (or has access if they want) to the Internet. In many societies, we see most people between the ages of 12 and 60 clutching smartphones, which are really computers that also happen to be telephones. It is not uncommon in the United States for 3- and 4-year-olds to have their favorite websites. Surveillance technologies track and identify people walking the streets of cities all over the world, while GPS records where people are 24 hours a day. All of this happened so fast—essentially in less than one generation—yet *incrementally* with new dependencies on computing technology introduced into our lives literally almost on a monthly or yearly basis that we forget how much changed. It happened so fast that we have not had an opportunity to step back to understand what computing means to humanity's existence and yet humans are an introspective species that likes to think about things.

If you are between the ages of, say, 25 and 50, this is a survival guide for you. If you are between the ages of 51 and roughly 75, it is a fun read and useful for giving you meaning that enhances your sense of self-worth, if older, a glimpse at what your grandchildren are about to experience, a peek at the arc of your family's future—it is why you want to be old enough to dance at your granddaughter's wedding. If you are under 25, well, this is about your future, but I realize you will probably only read this if a professor, older relative, or your manager puts it in front of you and insists that you devote a couple of hours meeting your future. Nobody will be more affected by what is in this book than your generation.

I did not want to write this book. I have other research that I am pursuing as a business and technology historian that are both interesting and I think relevant. But, as I entered my 70th decade of life, having observed what was happening with computers for forty years, computing, information technology, or whatever else you wish to call it, I concluded that too many people were too focused on the widgets, their smartphones and tablets as individuals, and corporations on hybrid cloud applications and supply chain management processes. If we stepped back just a few steps for just a little while, we can see that computing is a far bigger deal, one that transcends narrower issues. It involves privacy, an issue I am concerned with, role of computers in shaping or eliminating jobs, and effects on my grandchildren who hover so much over tablets. It concerns the future in which we have to ask who controls what: the computer us or we the computer? The bigger questions are about who runs the planet and how humans as a species evolve. These sound like mega issues, and they are, and I believe individuals have a role to play in how people evolve, precisely because of their access to computing. The issue of the role of computing on Earth is right up there, nearly with breathing air to sustain life, the existence and role of God in human values, and the evolution of climate change and its effects on life. This is pretty heady stuff if you are trying to pay bills every month, worrying about whether some company is going to lay you off because a computer can do your job or someone in a faraway country is less expensive.

I think humanity, as a species, does not understand how important computing is to its survival and success. That is why I set aside more mundane projects, shared my thinking, and offered my nearly half century of observations for whatever they are worth. I hope others do the same, as I have learned that I do not always have the right answers. I am confident, however, that I know many of the issues to raise, what alarm bells to ring. I also offer up for your consideration some "connecting the dots" insights.

Raising issues is important, because most people reasonably do not sit around and think about the nature of current and future computing or of the technology's possible implications. But they should, so this book is for them, but also for the experts in computing and artificial intelligence (AI) and the vendors who sell us those wonderfully magical digital toys that clutter our lives with fun and work. I have calibrated to the best of my ability what level of detail we mortals need to get about our lives as parents, employees, managers, leaders, Luddites, social creatures, and thoughtful, even piously decent people. It is difficult to address what over seven billion people should know, and I realize this is a hopeless objective. Or is it? Go back to how I began this preface, reporting how many people engage with computing, whether they like it or not. We don't get to vote on that; it is our reality, so we need to know enough to do enough to make life happy and productive enough. So how should we proceed?

I believe this book has to be more essay than tome to ponder the influence of computing on humans. It is an exercise in thinking about digital things in a big picture way. How humanity developed, encountered, and used computers is a large topic, so to do the job right should reasonably require a very fat book, which is exactly what this is not. For one thing, to make the subject accessible to people with too little time to read and yet an important topic to consider, a short book is in order. For another, to truly understand a subject, humans need clarity—the elevator answer when properly expressed—in order to understand the important issues, the touch points, of a topic that they can further track and dig into. We are discovering this fact about how humans learn, which is why many scholarly presses now publish really short books on big topics that boil an issue down to its essence on which a reader can add on as much detail as they want. Starting with a fat book simply can confuse or add too many facts and thus risk hiding clarity and wisdom. That is why this is a short book about when humans used computers back in the twentieth and early twenty-first centuries and what that experience possibly means for our future.

It is based, however, on my encounters with computing. It is simply one person's point of view, a reflection of how computing's events of the late twentieth century affected one of its users. Critics may complain that I should have included discourses on all manner of sidebar issues involving information technology (IT) and its physical forms, that I should have engaged with specific authors about the evolution of computer science, artificial intelligences, the "singularity" when people and machines become one, theological implications (Do we need God if we all evolve into computers?), today's parents fretting over their children spending too much time engaging with their screens, and so forth. When you write a short book, all of that vast literature—and by my estimation, it consists of over 100,000 books and millions of articles—has to be subsumed under the covers of the short conversation. Priorities and hard decisions have to be made.

However, as any diligent student of a topic can attest, one can examine a great deal of material in nearly a half century—thousands of books and articles—speak to and listen at hundreds of conferences, engage colleagues at work, and interact with the materials at hand. That is what I have done. After all that activity, what does it mean? What insights have tumbled around in my mind to be explained? This book—the extended essay—addresses such questions. My experience suggests others have the same questions about their own personal encounters with computing, so this book can be seen as a journey taken together to form opinions about the meaning and role of computers in our lives. As a result, numerous footnotes, lengthy quotes, and bibliographic eye candy that so normally grace any serious books are missing here. We will travel light on this exploratory trip through information, information technology, and the widgets that so clutter our lives. For those not acknowledged in this text, my apologies, but you are not ignored, just added into the soup of tacit knowledge accumulated over time.

More specifically, our purpose is to argue the case for several ideas. Computers are important additions to the human tool kit. Many people believe we live in some sort of Information or Computer Age—although I argue that we really don't—but for the time being, let's agree that we occupy a period enveloped by all manner of computing, both good and bad, large and small, difficult and simple to use. Computers are also *temporary* because of their ability to be shaped and be used in so many ways—what experts call a "general-purpose technology" as stand-alone devices: large mainframes (servers), laptops and PCs, and handheld smartphones that soon will seem as large mementos emblematic of our time just as cars with big fins bespoke 1950s–1960s. These technologies are increasingly becoming part of the Earth's environment, of the world we live in at work and at home, as part of any device we use. These already have arrived; think about our programmable coffee makers or fancy video doorbells that tells our smartphone who is calling us or the digital sensors that instruct our home furnaces when to turn on.

In time, computing's capabilities will be a part of our social and physical DNA. As a reminder of the obvious, our DNA and that of every living creature are the true databases and software that made life possible through the ages. Our existence as humans is based on DNA, and if computing contributes to that, then we can argue that computers will increasingly be one of the most important influences affecting the nature of humanity's form and way of functioning over the next several centuries. This would be a development ranked up there with climate conditions and living on other planets. That computing/DNA nexus is a powerful idea whose possibility no longer can be ignored, even if it feels more like science fiction than real science. However, increasingly today, sociologists, political scientists, media experts, and historians are viewing society as a massive information ecosystem, almost as an extended living creature in which the Internet contributes to this worldview. So the idea is already out of the bottle.

A second idea we explore is that today's computing that is made up of hardware, plastic, rubber, metal, and software (the latter also comprising of electrons, magnetized physical objects, and electricity) may someday be integrated into our physical beings, be part of our bodies and possibly of other life forms. If this technology makes the leap from metal and plastic to biological mass, which is possible as it compresses to the level of atoms, that turn of events would represent a fundamental leap in the evolution in how living creatures continue to adapt to their ever-changing environment. In such a scenario, computers become an intimate part of their environment, just as do trees, oxygen, and sunshine. It would be right up there with humans gaining the capacity to think consciously, speak, and walk upright. We do not fully understand the implications, let alone have consensus, but the potential for rapid transformation is there. But, humans have already proven they can adapt their bodies to fundamentally new conditions in a matter of a few generations. They are not finished transforming.

Will computing then help shape life in living creatures? What influence do we have on the features of that capability? While we do not know the answers to those two questions, we can at least begin to ponder them. That we dare ask them already suggests how important computing is to humanity. Often fundamental questions of human existence never are satisfactorily answered but take a half millennium or more to understand. For one thing, we can begin to appreciate that our human-centered view of so much—what theologians and scientists often describe as our anthropomorphic view of the world—will be challenged. As life and the world we live in change, thanks to computing embedded in "everything," will our reality be replaced or be rivaled by another paradigmatic lens, not seen through the eyes of humans?

To illustrate the point, a human-centered view of religion has a divine God who, according to Christian, Islamic, and Judaic faiths, is largely a man; children are shown pictures of an elderly vigorous older gentleman with a white beard or a kindly looking young man—Jesus—who also has a mother (Mary a female human), even an earthly human father (Joseph), and a heavenly father (the same elder with white beard). Buddha is pictured in humanlike form. And so it goes throughout much religion. The issue of the possible decline of our anthropomorphic perspective is more than just a loss of intellectual power and dominance over ideas and observations. It possibly signals the emergence of some other world view stimulated by ever-smarter computers which, again thinking anthropomorphically, computer scientists and AI experts believe will be as smart (or more) than humans in the second half of the twenty-first century. Hmm? What can all that mean?

So there is much to think about that goes far beyond discourses about blockchains and bitcoins, children's screen times, AI in global supply chains, the Internet of Things (IoT), how to download an app to our smartphones and to stream a TV program to whatever device we favor, or what privacy issues have ensnared Facebook or Google. Computing is increasingly becoming central to the existence of humans.

I propose to start discussing crucial topics through the medium of several short chapters. Following our human modern way of thinking, an introduction sets the table, by explaining our collective already considerable expertise in computing, yes about you dear reader. Then Chapter 1 defines what computing is today, while Chapter 2 will be the world's shortest history lesson on how we got to where we are now. Spoiler Alert: I will offend many hundreds of historians, technologists, and journalists who have done wonderful research on this topic as I purposefully fail to acknowledge them by name and oversimplify their work, since we don't have time to do more than wave at them as we jog through nearly a century of computer history.

Chapters 3 and 4 move into the issues of human-centered views of computing: computing as comparable to or replacement of the human brain. This is where we converse about AI. It is when we discuss the part machines and sensors play as physical parts of our global information ecosystem. Chapter 5 speculates—ponders—how we might see the end of the Information Age as we humans understand it, as everything has embedded in it computing first developed by people, but latter by who knows what. Computing as part of all life's DNA would represent both a novel development in life forms and a return to business as usual in the evolutionary schemes of things. Chapter 6 comes full circle to begin answering a simple but powerful question: So what? What implications can we draw from our discussions in prior chapters? Chapter 7 continues that discussion, setting us up for the last chapter which proposes a reshaping of our definition of our species and how we interact with computing. It also provides specific advice on how to keep up with this ever-changing technology.

The questions and issues raised can be discomforting, especially the possibility that computing morphs into the natural world, although we are a ways off from such a transformation. It could also possibly never happen. That we dare raise such issues, however, suggests that computing itself and its effects on human life right now gives this technology a gravitas we would not have dared to impose before the wide diffusion of the Internet, beginning in the mid-1990s. The concerns and issues that we must engage with transcend generations. Aging baby boomers and millennials share the same concerns, questions, and destinies as co-members of the same species occupying the same planet. Differentiating among generations misses the point. What I think and do as a boomer affects my children and grandchildren, just as what my children do impacts my life and that of their children. It's time for a more comprehensive species-wide view of what is happening.

I would like to thank my publisher for publishing this book, and particularly my editor, Wayne Wheeler, who has been a long-serving enthusiastic supporter of my investigations into information and computing. The production team at Copernicus has done its job well. Two experts on computing—Jeffrey Yost and Gerard Alberts—were instrumental in supporting this project when it came to my editor. You, I, and all three and their colleagues have traveled a long journey across decades to an understanding of computing, happily converging on this project. My views are my own, however, and do not necessary reflect those of my publisher or the Charles Babbage Institute at the University of Minnesota.

Minneapolis, MN, USA   James W. Cortada

Introduction: Why Listen to Me? Why You Should Take Seriously Your Own Knowledge of Computers

I am not a theologian, philosopher, or computer scientist. I have struggled with Microsoft software, laptops, and my Apple computer just like the rest of you. I still cannot keep up with all the functionality of my smartphone, which I still think is a really dumb device, and I prefer paper books to e-books. But I am a product of the twentieth and early twenty-first centuries, just like you. I have been around computers for a long time and have had to explain to many people what they do and their effects. I encountered my first computer system in the basement of a dorm in college in the mid-1960s—an IBM 1400 system comprising of multiple machines—and it looked the part we all think of: lots of devices the size of big kitchen refrigerators, made noisy by whirling components and tapes and all made out of metal. I played Hangman and Baseball on it. After college, it was off to graduate school where I picked up a Ph.D. in Modern History.

That turned out to be only a momentary escape from computers, because I then began a long career at IBM, where for nearly four decades and for between 50 and 70 hour workweeks, I observed how companies in over a dozen industries deployed computers through my roles in sales and consulting, explaining to hundreds of executives and even more managers and their employees what these machines could do and the possible consequences of their deployment. Along the way, I studied, wrote, and spoke about the history of computing and their current applications. I sometimes felt like the mid-nineteenth-century rebel Lutheran theologian/philosopher, Søren Kierkegaard, who struggled with what Christianity was all about by writing extensively almost every day of his adult life about it. In my case, I was trying to understand the technology while implementing it and watching it change form and impact in real time. Like the Lutheran, I ended up having written a shelf full of books about the use and history of computing before I even retired from IBM.

Computers changed me. For one thing, after being at IBM for two decades, I began to realize that we—IBM, its customers, and scholars—were spending too much time fixated on the hardware, the machines, and not enough on the software, ignoring the ultimate purpose of computers: their production and use of information. It was always about the answers these technologies pumped out. It took my writing a three-volume history of how computers changed the work of entire industries for me to tumble onto—understand—the central task of computers: they augmented the work of humans by taking over some of their work. Talk to a help desk at one's telephone company, and you are handled by a computer; do the same when inquiring about when a package is going to be delivered, and again, another conversation with a computer, while a third one is deciding whether you qualify for a home mortgage or a new credit card. Today, if you look up a product, for days, you will be inundated with advertisements for it on your Facebook account. You have encountered more computers that have made decisions about you. Facebook routinely collects thousands of pieces of data about you. Evidence is mounting that up to 60 percent of what we read on the Internet was written by a piece of software, not a person. In short, we have come full circle from when computers were first created, when they were invented for one primary purpose: to create and help manage the use of information.

Upon leaving IBM at the end of 2012, I turned my energy to studying how people used information, treating computers as support actors—tools if you wish—but with information always the central player. More articles, talks, and books were my way, like the Danish theologian, to sort out what computing was about, its importance and role. To be in the arena tangling with the central technology of our time was relevant, important, and, in the end, fascinating. Like you and especially those engaged with computers or lived during their arrival and diffusion, much changed, all incrementally, but quickly.

For one thing, when I was a teenager in the early 1960s, there were only an estimated 6,000 to 7,000 computers worldwide; today, there are so many that we do not know how many exist. You may have a hundred in your home if you have digital alarm clocks, TVs, a microwave oven, two cars in the garage, a lawn mower, plus the usual digital devices, such as smartphones, laptops, and iPads. They shrank from being the size of refrigerators to devices capable of being injected into your bloodstream. There is even "smart dust," other computers with the ability to store and manipulate data in tiny sensors, and intelligent drones that look like small insects. Add in magnetizable liquids and tiny communications with the ability to store data in individual atoms, and you have humankind on the verge of being able to track every step and action taken by every human being (plus many animals) for their entire lives.

Let me turn to the second part of this introduction's title—Why You Should Take Seriously Your Own Knowledge of Computers—because my experience is not unique. For one thing, tens of thousands of people have written books and articles and have made presentations at technical conferences; millions attended such sessions, and tens of millions of you work in the world of information technology as computer scientists, programmers, and machine operators and still others manufacturing devices and hundreds of millions using them as central features of their daily work. No country is isolated from these realities. Go to a Benedictine monastery atop some European mountain and you will encounter laptops, smartphones, and online library catalogs; visit a village in India that recently gained access to electricity and you will see tablets and smartphones. London's officials have been complaining for well over a decade that computers are consuming so much electricity that the city runs the risk of not having enough of this kind of energy with which to operate. The movement of some computing out of London to the continent as a result of Brexit concerns does not end the concern. The point is most people under the age of 65 know a great deal about computers, and as one of them, you should acknowledge that fact.

Yes, you know more about computers or, more accurately, about computing than you probably give yourself credit for, which is one reason this book already should resonate with you. This also means that you can read it with the critical eye of an expert. Your collective biography goes something like this. As a species, you began to hear about these new devices in the 1950s and 1960s, most did not encounter them at work in the 1970s (except for a few million), but then by the end of the 1980s had. Personal computers flooded the world by tens of millions in the 1980s. Their appearance forced you to learn, first conceptually, what was a computer; second, what it could be used for; third, how to use it; and fourth, why. You learned incrementally about this technology and by the end of that decade had formed opinions about it based on personal "hands-on" experience. Some of you, in addition, did too through the use of large mainframes and interacting with these through terminals that almost looked like PCs, but were not. You called them "dumb terminals," or "green screens," while PCs soon displayed colored images and could be used in so many new ways.

You learned new words and concepts: "computer chips," "operating systems," "programming languages," "online," "spread sheets," and "e-mail." Games took on a new meaning, no longer flat pieces of cardboard with plastic pieces to move about on them; you now could simulate being a pilot in some of the most popular online games of the 1980s–1990s. Your children and, for some, grandchildren made online gaming one of the most widely used forms of computing after 2010.

You also learned how to judge the value and functions of new devices that had computing in them, and you did this with confidence: digital cameras, programmable television sets, use of the Internet for information searches and then to make purchases, and so forth. How do we know you had confidence? Because economists and entire industries tracked how quickly you embraced new forms of computing. They learned that every time a new form of computing came along, you acquired these faster than the previous generation of information technology. That is how we can largely explain the success of properly run companies offering these new devices, such as Apple, and services too, such as e-Bay, Amazon, and Google.

Many experts like to argue that the behavior of different generations varies in their use of computing. They will argue that really old people use these devices far less than really young people. That certainly was true in the late 1990s and the first decade of the new century. But it is an old paradigm that no longer makes as much sense as before. I knew a 103-year-old who used an Apple tablet because it afforded her the ability to project larger print versions of her local newspaper. Nursing homes are full of PCs, tablets, and smartphones. Most of their residents have been around computers for decades, in fact many for longer than their 20's something grandchildren. True, each new generation was exposed to computing at an earlier age and to more portable varieties, offering more functions than their predecessors, but we have reached a point where differentiating between generations is increasingly mis-leading. People in their 70s use their smartphones for the same purposes as others in their 30s. Both generations look up information, play games, watch TV pro-grams, place orders, and engage with friends and family using Facebook and other social media. All adult generations reinforce his or her political views with fake and real news, and everyone seems to check the weather.

Older users have the experience over younger ones of having seen the technology evolve. Along the way, they saw devices shrink in size and cost, while designers massively increased their ability to collect, store, sort, present, and analyze informa-tion for and about you. All that happened in one lifetime. Talk to computer scientists and they enthusiastically tell you that they see no end in sight to the continued evo-lution of this general-purpose technology or its miniaturization while expanding its ability to collect and process ever-increasing amounts of data.

In short, you are more expert about the technology than you might have thought, especially about how best to use it. Yet, if you are bewildered by all of this and con-cerned about what it means, especially after I hinted that perhaps the human race would evolve again because of this technology, then imagine how I feel being close up confronting these machines for a half century. But even more to the point, it's due to your prior experience that you are entitled to feel bewildered, because you know enough that you should be puzzled. Acting like an expert, you appreciate the need to understand the context of what you are experiencing.

I referred earlier to the idea that millions of people were learning new computer-oriented words; your latest are probably "AI" and "cloud," maybe even "5G." But I have some bad news: just as the technology kept changing over the past half century, so too did the vocabulary that we used to describe it. Old fat printed dictionaries of computer terms had to be replaced with new ones, of course, while writers had to update their lingo. Remember when we spoke about *computers*? Now they are called *servers*. My first book had EDP (electronic data processing) in its title when published in 1980, its sequel a few years later spoke of management information systems (MIS) in 1984, in yet another in 2001, about "the new digital economy," then in a later one in 2015, I had to speak about "information ecosystems." This constant churn in how you and I speak about computers is not going to end any time soon.

Take, for example, the word *machine*. It may soon no longer reflect what these are. Today, the vast cost for computing and for their "care and feeding" is not for hardware (computers and other devices) and their electricity, rather for their soft-ware—something you and I have never seen—as these are largely electrical impulses traveling through our world with only their output made visible to humans on screens and as reports. Increasingly, sensors, which gather more data than humans do and travel through the Internet, don't bother to deal with such living beings. People just get in the way and are too slow to handle the volume of information, so they "talk" to other sensors and computers as they go about their work.

Welcome to your future, to that of every descendant you will ever have. Now you understand why I argue that nothing matches computing except perhaps life itself and the physical environment we live in. No human invention since the discovery of fire, or the wheel, and the development of our ability to think and talk is perhaps as important as the computer. Let us begin with a frustration: the word *computer* may also no longer suffice to explain what we are talking about, yet I have not seen a better term. Even my clever colleagues at IBM who have been dealing with computers since the 1940s have not come up with a better one. "A tool for modern times" may have been the closest they got to in the 1980s when describing personal computers. "Artificial intelligence" is very much off the mark if, as I am thinking, computing's "intelligence" becomes integrated in life forms it no longer is artificial. "Cognitive computing" is borderline incomprehensible except that it does clearly suggest that computers learn from their data and experiences—a hugely important evolution in computing that gets them closer to becoming part of living creatures. What makes computing artificial is that we think of it in anthropomorphic terms outside our bodies, even if augmenting what our brains do.

If you think, perhaps, that we are not so innocent as to think of computers as almost humanlike, I present as Exhibit A our recently available devices that we talk to. Let me introduce you to two things who are already close intimates to millions: Alexa and her cohort, Siri. Alexa is the name given to an Amazon device that responds to human voice queries and commands to look up information on the Internet or, if programmed to communicate with household devices, to turn on and off lights, television sets, and play music. It has a friendly, non-threatening non-judgmental female voice. We think of this device as anthropomorphic—a female. Siri is Apple's version of Alexa, except "she" can talk to you from your smartphone and like Alexa has increased "her" ability to engage in humanlike conversations. They are not alone. GPS-based voice-activated driving instructions are also humanlike. What automobile driver today doesn't ask such questions as, "What does she say to do next?" "Where does she want us to turn?" These driving systems also come in male voices, in many languages, speaking with different accents. We shall see many more such devices before too long. Developers of computing are shaping them into humanlike creatures, and already some are remaking themselves—the cognitive computers with AI mentioned above. So, humans let's confront our possible destiny.

Contents

Chapter 1
What Is Computing?

Seventy-five years ago answering this question was easy. A Hungarian mathematician named John von Neumann laid it out in a short report in the mid-1940s that said essentially a computer had three parts: input, which is data and instructions collected and sent to a processor, second, that part of the machine that did something with the input, such as adding or subtracting numbers, and third, output, the act of pushing the results to a printer, punch cards or later onto magnetic tape and even later to magnetic storage. His ideas became known as the Von Neumann Architecture and a half century later, it was still essentially the big picture description of a computer: three parts, which could consist of a bunch of specialized machines, such as one to punch holes into stiff cards, the computer itself (processor, later server), and all manner of output devices, connected together with electrical wires and cables, and all managed by software much like traffic signals or police directing the flow of vehicles through a community.

While the functions he described are still the same, answering the question became harder, because, too, at its essence the computer was one of those general-purpose technologies mentioned in the Preface. Unlike a hammer or screwdriver, which remained essentially the same (if in different sizes), computers did not. That is why one can walk around with a computer in their hand—a smartphone—that has far more capacity to hold information and to process data than did any computer built in the first several decades of its existence. That reality leads us to the first part of the answer: computers are highly diverse, flexible devices that can take in information, do something with it, and then present the output either to humans or to other machines (i.e., computers, traffic lights, your automobile's motor, or Alexa to answer your questions).

It all began with humans trying to "crunch" numbers faster and more accurately, often using women called computers (i.e., people who compute or calculate answers). The earliest machines were used to tabulate numbers, such as to count inventory or project the orbit of the moon, and so required much data that the machine could read and ability to do simple mathematics, later calculus and geometry. Over time, as the cost of storing data declined and the capacity to store

© Springer Nature Switzerland AG 2020
J. W. Cortada, *Living with Computers*,
https://doi.org/10.1007/978-3-030-34362-0_1

information grew, computers could handle text—information—often in combination with numbers and images. This leads us to a second answer to our question: computers can collect, analyze, compute (process) "machine readable data" (information) and present the results, which is why computer scientists and business users refer to computers as processors doing data processing.

With that functionality established and 75 years of computer developers reducing the size of these machines, increasing their ability to do more things with data, and people increasingly relying on these with which to go about their work, these information engines went from being behemoths in "data centers" to becoming ever smaller ones that could physically be "distributed" around an organization to the private preserves of clusters of engineers or accounting departments, for example, all under their personal control. These connected to mainframes in the big data centers, "talking" to each other, that is to say, sending information back and forth, often over telephone lines. That connectivity created an information infrastructure within an organization upon which people became increasingly dependent with which to work.

So, that leads to a third answer: computers became the backbone of electronic information infrastructures. The process continued with people putting PCs on their desks (beginning in the mid-1970s), laptops in their bags and cars (1980s), and smartphones in their purses (2010s). Simultaneously, people embedded this technology inside non-computer machines, such as automobile engines to improve gas mileage, and in huge manufacturing machines to improve or simplify operations, all beginning in the 1970s. Precision, accuracy, safety, and volume of activities began to be managed by computers. Today, computers are *the* governing technologies in everything from space ships to your programmable coffee pot.

Computing is the act of using computers (hardware and software) to gather, calculate, analyze, store, protect, and present information faster and more accurately than can a human, and most often, too, less expensively. Computing has become a catch phrase for the hardware and software, the communications needed to move information from one place to another (such as what the Internet does), and what we do with this kluge of IT. Asking your smartphone for directions to a restaurant involves computing, so too calculating the flight path of a missile from North Korea aimed at Japan. How some of this came about will be discussed later, but for our purposes recognize what are the basic activities of a computer and that these boil down to collecting, crunching, and displaying information useful to us or to other machines.

Do computers process data—information—differently than humans? It is an important question because for the entire history of computers the design objectives were largely to make these machines act on our behalf as augmentations to the way we think and in the world of AI the aspiration to build machines that were as smart as humans. It turns out, however, that people and machines think differently. First, machines work faster than humans, processing billions and trillions of pieces of data in a second; we are really good at handling one piece of information in the same amount of time. Computers are clueless about what they are processing, but we humans understand what we are doing and so can quickly change course if the evidence suggests, because we are learning as we work. That is why computer scientists like to say that computers are really dumb; they can make mistakes a lot faster than any of us, and those can be expensive or deadly, as occurred in 2018 and 2019 with the crash of two Boeing 737 aircraft, which did not get it that the pilots really did not want to fly into the ground. The accidents were judged to be the result of faulty software unable to correct its own poor design. Bridging the gap between human capabilities and those of computers is a central agenda for computer scientists today.

Elegance in presenting this concept is not required; thousands of other writers have done that and their charts and texts are often spectacular, showing, for example, the evolution in the ability of a machine to do work growing at compound rates of 15–30 percent *per year* for decades, ditto about their capacity to store large quantities of information, and similarly how the costs of processing information have dropped by compound annual rates also in the 20 + percent for decades. It was not a snarky comment made by computer advertisements in the 1970s that if automotive manufacturers had been as productive in developing automobiles as were computer vendors that one could buy a Ferrari sports car for $5, today for pennies. In time humans will probably conclude that the evolution of computing in the late twentieth and early twenty-first centuries mimicked the development of human flight, for example, probably that computing evolved more dramatically than air transportation. Those readers who have flown on commercial flights between 1970 and 2020, and who ask why planes fly at the same speed as forty years ago understand.

In sum, computers come in all shapes and sizes, able to be embedded in anything that we want. That desire parallels a long-standing practice of people wrapping information around other objects. Think of cans of soup that as part of their label includes a recipe for using the product, our prescriptions that include on the side of the container instructions on use, or starting instructions for all manner of lawn care machinery. Tools, cooking utensils, small machinery, and many other devices also include instructions. Fathers all over the world facing the challenge of assembling a toy have found in its box the dreaded "some assembly required" message that included information on how to do that, hopefully in a language they understood. The new twist to this old practice of encasing objects with information is adding computing to the device so that it can take instructions from us, such as telling a microwave oven how long to "zap" cold food. Today one can ask Alexa how long the microwave oven should do that, even have "it" instruct it to do that.

The second feature of computing is that simultaneous to giving us instructions, for over 40 years they have been designed to control our interactions with computers and other processes, even physical access to buildings, requiring that we obey them. Being required to enter a password to access your bank account through an ATM is an example of this. Fail to do so and a computer will keep you away from your money. Fail to know the secret password to get into your work place, and you will sit outside until someone lets you in, even if you are the president of the company. More complicated versions of a computer's authority can be found when filling in information online on a form that, if you skip anything, causes the computer to not take any of your information or simply shuts you out of whatever was of interest to you. It is simply comparing what you put in with what information should have been provided and when a disconnect occurs, has been programmed to deny something to you. Von Neumann would have been pleased that his simple explanation continues to help us understand was is happening. If the computer was a conscious living creature, it would also be delighted, because after you blamed "the computer" and then began thinking about it, you would really have to charge the poor human programmer who did not write better software.

This leads to a third aspect of what is a computer: it is a device (system of various machines and software) that was designed by humans and evolves (so far) through their actions. Remember this last point as we travel through the rest of this book.

Chapter 2
How Did We Get Here?

People began using computers during World War II to decipher German military communications codes, which a generation of historians in the late 1970s recognized as one of a half dozen reasons why the Allies defeated Hitler. Computers have now been around so long that they have a rich history of their own, also now a second generation of historians documenting it. Gather a group of them into a room and you are guaranteed to have multiple points of view about how some historical event unfolded, which is now happening through a continuous flow of articles and books about the evolution of computing. It is becoming more evident that how we got from big machines to sensors in all manner of devices today is not one story, but several lines of development. These investigations suggest how other "high-tech" machines have and will develop, which is why it is worth a few pages to take a fast jog through the history of computing. It is a testament to the widespread use of computers that many observers assume (almost without saying so) that just about any "high-tech" machine is an extension of computing, because these are so saturated and controlled through the use of digital technologies.

There are four arcs in the development of computers. Think of an arc as a thesis, a point of view used to explain why something happened. In the early history of an event, or device, the single thesis approach is often used because initial evidence points to one explanation and it is also a convenient way to begin linking together strings of events. Only after that initial attempt and the subsequent discovery of more evidence do we realize the obvious: that nothing is simple, just as in other aspects of our lives. Answering this chapter's central question—How Did We Get Here?—now requires multiple answers. More than just new arcs that have become fashionable, these reflect more judicious and serious minded thinking about the importance of computing in the human experience.

© Springer Nature Switzerland AG 2020
J. W. Cortada, *Living with Computers*,
https://doi.org/10.1007/978-3-030-34362-0_2

How Humans Invented Computers

The first historical arc favored by historians and the pioneer engineers and scientists who developed these machines and software involves focusing on the technologies themselves, such as development of electrical components, computer chips, pieces of equipment, programming languages, software packages (like word processing or spreadsheet programs), and telecommunications. Technological perspectives on how computers came into being long dominated the way people viewed computers—an amazing history. Marketing and advertising folks promoted it too. One of my favorite tag lines comes from the cover of IBM's employee magazine, *Think*, from January/February 1976, which launched the entire issue's focus on technological history with, "It was to have been the nuclear age. It became the computer age." Pages of gorgeous photographs of machines and components followed. The magazine's writers argued that, "in the past quarter-century, the computer has moved from the margins of our existence into the center of our lives." Little did they realize how so that would become truer in the next quarter-century.

It is a twentieth century story with roots going back to the dawn of the previous century. With the availability of electricity in the 1840s and electrical components, such as vacuum tubes in the 1910s, transistors in the 1940s and computer chips in the 1960s, machines could be built to handle the coursing of electrons in combinations of pluses and minuses, zeroes and ones, to form instructions and data. As the components shrank in size, yet could do more, engineers and mathematicians developed programming languages that allowed people to write instructions and collect data these machines could use with other software embedded in the machines (later computer chips) to translate into the pulses of zeroes and ones that the hardware understood. The earliest machines had exotic names, such as ENIAC, EDVAC and Whirlwind. They were all one of a kind machines developed for government and academic use. Mass production did not come to computing until the mid-1950s. By then they were being named by model numbers; IBM's included such boring names as 7090, 650, and 1401. Not exciting, but these names distinguished one system from another.

Once the technology had advanced enough for commercial development, beginning in the early 1950s, they acquired new names such as UNIVAC, Defense Calculator, but also their numeric tag lines, such as the "IBM 650," "IBM 1400," and so forth. Between then and the end of the 1980s, hundreds of different models and sizes of mainframes appeared, and by the 1970s almost on a weekly basis peripheral equipment. The computer industry had well over two dozen major computer vendors. That count does not include the thousands of niche companies that developed peripheral equipment, such as printers, or software firms. By the end of the 1960s one could acquire three classes of computers: super computers (very large used for scientific and defense work), mainframes (the kind adopted by companies and government agencies to do clerical and business work called *applications*), and smaller more specialized devices called minicomputers. IBM dominated the mainframe piece of the technology and its market by the start of the 1960s and held onto that lead through the 1980s, while myriad vendors fought over the minicomputer market, such as Hewlett-Packard. Supercomputers remained a tiny segment all through the period.

Then a fundamental shift occurred in the history of computing technology involving the development of small devices that could sit on one's desk, that by the early 1980s were called personal computers, or just simply PCs. First introduced in the 1970s, and made possible by sufficient miniaturization of computer chips and memory to store information in these, a new market developed quickly. This is when Steve Jobs and Apple came into being, when Bill Gates established Microsoft to sell software to operate in this class of machines. By the end of the 1980s, people were buying tens of millions of PCs all over the world. The arc of computing's technical history is a story of further miniaturization of components that made the laptop possible by the early 1990s, portable phones at the same time for the similar reasons, then even smaller devices early in the new century better known as iPads and smartphones. Smart watches and other "wearables" are some of the most recent manifestations of the evolution of the technology.

Running parallel to the evolution of the hardware and software were technological innovations in telecommunications. When those two sets of technologies were married—computers and communications—computing went massively global and massive in capabilities, justifying the reason for our jog through computer history. Telegraph and telephone technologies originated in the nineteenth century with the first to transmit electrical pulses that could be converted into words through the translation of sequences of those electrical pulses, while telephones did the same for voices and that by the 1920s were transmitting pictures too. Many early computer developers had grown up with telephony or as radio hobbyists. With the arrival of commercially available computers and others for specialized military purposes by the mid-1950s the dream of somehow connecting these all up surfaced. That called for linking computers to each other via telephone lines. The technologists figured out how to accomplish that in the 1960s.

When combined with the ability to access specific pieces of information in a computer largely by way of a terminal connected by telephone to a computer, that combination made it possible for non-technical workers to use computers from all over an organization, not simply from down the hall from a large mainframe. Computing then exploded with growth in the 1970s and 1980s. During the second half of the 1980s PCs began communicating with each other and with mainframes and minicomputers. The key transition turned out to be giving computers the ability to share information with each other via telecommunications.

While that was occurring another line of development in telecommunications was underway in university, government, and company laboratories away from the public's view that in time became known as the Internet. Originally developed in the United States as a secure network for military and defense contractors to communicate that could not be destroyed by nuclear war, by the early 1980s it was being used by academics, too, on both sides of the Atlantic. Then in the early 1990s, Sir Tim Berners-Lee, a Brit working in Switzerland, developed a way to make communicating anthropomorphically over the Internet with the World Wide Web. Instead of text on a screen appearing like some ancient hieroglyphic language, people could use human languages—like English—to type texts on a normal typewriter-like keyboard used with their PCs.

By the dawn of the next century one could transmit over the Internet files, later photographs and other images, pay bills, advertise, and expound on any subject they wanted. This technological development made it possible to essentially connect every computer on Earth to every other one and to do the same for any machinery or object that had computing embedded in it. It was the combination of computing and telecommunications technologies that made the invention of "the computer" one of the more important inventions of humankind. It was a milestone event in technology and science. With these developments, in theory all people could communicate with any other human if they had their e-mail address.

It Took Money and Organizations to Make IT Possible

But that is not the only way to view the history of computing. A second perspective—arc—emphasizes the institutional support of universities, armies and other military branches, and most notably national governments. This point of view holds that by governments investing heavily in the development of computing's expensive and risky technologies between the 1940s and the end of the century it became possible for computers to be invented, improved, and used. They are correct, of course, because computer developers needed to be paid by someone to do this work. The demands of World War II launched the process, first by the British requiring machines that could quickly break German military communications codes, which led to their government investing in what became known as COLOSSUS computers. The Americans wanted to more accurately calculate artillery firing tables and improve precision bombing capabilities, invent atomic bombs, next do better weather forecasting and the design of airplanes by the early 1950s, all of which led to such machines as the ENIAC and Whirlwind.

The Cold War stimulated demand for computers to assist in the design of new generations of nuclear bombs, to build networks to identify incoming enemy missiles, guidance systems for the missiles themselves, and for space travel from the 1950s to the present. These projects were largely funded by the USSR and USA through the 1980s, and by the Americans afterwards, today by Russia and China as well. I am tempted to say these nations collectively invested trillions of dollars over the half-century following World War II, but we just do not know precisely how much since such budgets were shrouded in secrecy, but for sure hundreds of billions of dollars. These investments continue today for similar reasons. This facet of computing's history is relevant because now the Chinese and Russian governments are spending massively on such technological innovations as AI, disruption of the Internet, and in biologically-based systems, not just the United States.

In the case of Western Europe and the United States, but not the old Soviet Union, governments commissioned companies in data processing (such as IBM), electronics (such as GE), and in defense industries to do the heavy lifting of research and development by commissioning specific projects, such as the development of an air national defense network in the USA, known as SAGE. These companies then converted such government computers into commercial versions. IBM led the pack in doing this well, but also UNIVAC, GE, and RCA for a while. That is why the Americans were able to create a vibrant commercial computer industry by the late 1950s that proved larger and more advanced than anyone else's, even though the British had led the world in technical developments in the 1940s. The latter were unable to take the next step in their development because their nation could not afford to invest as extensively in creating the needed new machines as did the larger, richer United States. Affordability rapidly emerged as an obvious worldwide problem by the late 1950s when it became evident to even the most casual military or public official controlling budgets for such projects that this was going to be one of the most expensive technological developments in human history.

This tale of affordability should remind us that scale is an important consideration when discussing how to address climate change, the elimination of cancer or some other disease, or colonization of Space. Development of the computer was made possible by humankind having enough money *and* technological knowledge to do the required work to design, develop, build, sell, use, and maintain what was always seen as a complex technology. Mankind's projects also kept becoming more complex *and* expensive, too, as when they could not be carried out unless computing already existed, such as the development of hydrogen nuclear bombs or space ships. Today computer-driven satellites point out the location and extent of wild fires at the Artic or in the Amazon jungles. All require the accumulation of sufficient knowledge, funding, and demand to undertake.

Computers Were Put to Good Use

A third arc—call it another thesis—argues that computers would not have amounted to much unless they could do practical things that organizations valued, referred to as *applications*. Economists called this aspect of computing the demand side of the story, what customers wanted from their government's R&D investments and more directly, from suppliers, such as IBM, Apple, or Microsoft. In the spirit of transparency, in the early 2000s, I advocated strongly for this perspective to receive more attention from historians than their dominant practice of studying the supply side of the story of engineers doing great things and governments supplying the funds for their work. Other historians expressed similar interest, expanding their work to include examining how people used computers, not just documenting the work of companies and governments, engineers, and computer scientists.

The logic runs as follows: In each era of computers, as developers went from one innovation to another, they had in mind specific uses for this technology that shaped their designs. For example, if banks wanted check processing automated using computers, they commissioned the construction of special machines that could physically handle, read, sort, and tabulate data from paper checks and update account files. That behavior began in the 1950s. When people bought PCs in large quantities in the 1980s it was because they had what came to be known as "killer apps," uses that made these machines attractive, such as word processing (typing text) and spreadsheet software, later the ability to transmit email. We buy new smartphones from Apple because each new generation of these devices can do things earlier ones could not, such as take better photographs, longer videos, offer greater data security, and so forth. GPS and photography were some of the earliest killer apps for such phones. In the 1950s it was the ability to do massive amounts of accounting and financial work and later in combination with scanners and other data collecting devices for depositing into computers information these could read, store, use quickly all far cheaper than human clerks.

As organizations came to rely on computers to do one then a few applications, they became increasingly dependent on this technology with which to do their work to such an extent that they could never revert back to pre-computer processes. Organizations made incremental changes to their computer infrastructures and to their applications (work practices) as the technology improved, better software came along, computing products made it possible to lower operating costs, or to do new things. Over time, users learned how to acquire new computers and how best to use them, moving from lack of confidence and hesitancy in the 1950s and 1960s to massive dependency on them within one generation, that is to say, by the end of the 1980s.

Note the enormous flexibility in how these systems were shaped, ranging from the big mainframes favored by large centralized organizations to the tiny smartphones we clutch. These machines and their software could also be made into highly specialized machines. Industrial robots that could paint automobiles is a good example, so too minicomputers encased in huge machines that made toilet paper or newsprint, or smaller ones in ATMs. It is that flexibility that made it possible to think of computers as "general-purpose" technologies. Combine imagination, enough funding, and very rapid transformation in the individual technical components (parts) and you begin to understand why it was possible to use these systems for so many purposes.

As a result, how companies and government agencies organized and operated changed fundamentally. By the end of the 1990s it was becoming clear to managers and economists that investments in computing were increasing the productivity of people and organizations; that individuals were relying incrementally on increasing amounts of information with which to make decisions; and that what they were able to do had evolved because of their ever growing dependency on computers now woven into the fabric of their daily work. I want to emphasize the notion of *incrementally*, because there was no Computer Revolution. If you were a manager, would you rather commit to spending, say, ten million U.S. dollars on one computer project in one fell swoop, or instead one million dollars per year over 10 years? Which option poses less risk to your company and to your personal career, given that the technologies involved kept changing and declining in cost? So while the media always spoke about revolutions and rapid changes, users of computers made evolutions, not revolutions.

Risk was the hidden darkness behind the story of massive adoption of computing. Back in the early 1980s, I warned general managers who were just beginning to oversee ever-bigger IT projects writing that, "All projects have risks and costs. The longer something takes to get completed, the more it costs and the later it is before benefits are enjoyed." No two projects had the same risks, and I observed that, "the bigger the task, the greater the risk of doing everything as originally planned." Then as now, novel uses of the technology were always shrouded by the unknown and since today we continue to implement new uses for IT as the technology continues to evolve the problems identified in the 1980s remain a constant in the life of any digital project.

That is why I, like so many others using older IT tools, am writing this book with a 7 year old release of Microsoft Word, but also because I don't have the time to learn how to use the latest release of this software. Furthermore, you know in its earliest stages every new release of a piece of software is going to have some problems. So, I wait a few months for others to work out the bugs. Like everyone else, I just as soon only embrace incrementally new word processing functions, such as when my publisher says I have to change my software so that her production department can work with my manuscript, which, of course, is prepared using a PC, unlike my first book which I wrote on a manual typewriter and sent to the editor as a stack of paper, not as an email attachment, like today.

IT Was First and Foremost All About Creating and Using Information

One could have reasonably concluded that with these three arcs in the development of computers that we knew how it all came about and why these were important. But we would be wrong. There is yet another arc of the story only just becoming obvious, thanks to the research of library and book historians, social media (a killer app on the Internet) experts, computer scientists, biologists, and a few historians of computing, including myself. The emerging arc was, perhaps, ultimately the most obvious in hindsight: the purpose of computers was to facilitate society's creation and use of information. Perhaps it took a half-century for the technology to be born and for humans to figure out what to do with it. Certainly there had been doubts all along about the value of using computers and uncertainties about their applications. Economists criticized the faith put in computers for a while by challenging the technology's defenders with snarky comments that they could not see the productivity gains in the statistics they normally gathered; in time they would learn that they were counting the wrong things.

Nobody wanted to be the first to use a computer in a different way. Cost justification remained a magician's shibboleth to many for decades. Writing proposals for the acquisition of new computer systems and uses seemed a dark art, a form of near fiction and persuasion yet to be studied by professors of great literature. Defenders of the technology had to constantly explain the "how" and "why;" one of those, James Martin, tried with over 70 books. By the early years of the next century it was coming together: computing was about society's production and use of information.

We should have known better, because as early as 1948 an MIT mathematician, Norbert Wiener, created the word *cybernetics*, which he used to bring together his years of studying mathematics, physics, medicine, and ballistics into a slim volume by the same name and subtitled *or Control and Communication in the Animal and Machine.* Cybernetics originated in Greek meaning steersman. Professor Wiener argued that the human nervous system and computers could be seen similarly as communications and control in physiological systems and machines. Perhaps he wrote the book a half-century too early, although it helped early computer designers think about their inventions' purposes. The link to human and biological feedback loops—how living creatures sense their world and respond to it—involved one fundamental medium: information. But with so many computers now protruding into our lives armed with so much research having been done about the human brain, nervous systems in all manner of living creatures, and concerning their use of information, historians, scientists, librarians, sociologists, and media experts began to see the world as one large mass of information handling. Computers were now viewed as the handmaidens of societies using information. Information was now the leading star of the human play, less so computers, which were now the ubiquitous supporting actors in the human drama. It took the rapid diffusion of the Internet worldwide in less than two decades for this insight to become obvious.

So today, scholars and pundits are off studying how people use information. Often they see information as the glue holding society together, the use of which constitute the bulk of the tasks performed by workers and pleasure seekers. Sometimes human reliance on information requires use of digital tools, such as computers or smartphones, at other times merely human conversation or reading, and, dare we still say it, a book, although even that medium comes in e-book formats through various digital tools. We can anticipate that Alexa will tell bedtime stories to our grandchildren, freeing up grandparents from participating in the information feedback loop that had joyfully facilitated bonding generations and families together for eons. Societies were now seen as aggregates of information, regardless of language or location.

Computers were postured as both having emerged as what a group of historians called "the Information Machine" and as now offering a path—a bridge—to society's future. IBM executives could run around speaking about "cognitive computing," while the old as yet undelivered promises of artificial intelligence could now be lauded as on society's cusp of really being delivered. This new arc—thesis—is heady stuff as it bristles with an even more urgent anthropomorphic potency than Alexa could ever offer in her (its) current beer-can shaped form. So, we are now knowledge workers, communities of practice, all living in an Information Age (even though we know it had always been an information age for any living creature). Computing, like the air we breathe, is now part of the digital plumbing of modern society. The technology had come a long way since just being concepts in the minds of clever people such as Alan M. Turing in the 1930s, radio ham operators in

Philadelphia, chess players and mathematicians working in war torn England at Bletchley House, or Professor Wiener.

How Computers Spread Around the World So Quickly

How we got here is a story that cannot end with these four explanations about the creation and uses of computing, even though it should be obvious by now that each was simultaneously in play for decades, each ebbing and flowing in importance. We still have the remaining question historians ask: How did so many computers spread so fast around the world? By looking at the emergence of computers on a country-by-country basis several patterns become evident. First, the original technology and support for its development occurred most sufficiently in the United States and Great Britain in the 1940s and 1950s. Second, tiny groups of engineers in most European countries west of the Iron Curtain tinkered with building one-of-a-kind systems in the 1940s and early 1950s, modeling their designs on British and American ones. Then, the Soviets began doing the same, but decided they could move faster in the late 1960s by simply mimicking American designs, most spectacularly IBM's.

In the 1970s and 1980s computing spread across all of Europe, in major industrial centers and capital cities in Latin America, and later into urban centers in southeast China. Japan became an extensive user of computers in the late 1950s. By the mid-1970s its native computer industry had emerged as a major competitor to IBM and other American and European computer manufacturers, selling such technology on both sides of the Atlantic. The arrival of PCs in large quantities in the 1980s made computing dramatically less expensive, hence more affordable around the world, notably in southern Europe, across large swaths of Southeast Asia, and in many parts of Latin America and South Africa. The spread of the Internet around the world, beginning in the 1990s, coupled with the arrival of smartphones, essentially made computing ubiquitous worldwide by 2015. Some Africans can buy an Apple knockoff phone for as little as $50 delivered from China, while we Americans are asked to pay as much as $1000 for an authentic Apple product.

What drove this fast diffusion were declining costs for such devices, improvements in the ease of use of these technologies, effective marketing and selling of such products, and literate societies supplied with the necessary infrastructures needed to support their acquisition and use. Other necessary prerequisites increasingly became available, too. These included steady supplies of electricity, incomes and rich-enough economies that could support the purchase of all manner of information technologies, rising levels of education, and not to be overlooked, the changing natures of work and play into more technologically dependent and cerebral forms to justify their use. As the number of people familiar with the technology increased, while simultaneously its evolution simplified, momentum grew. A Taiwanese teenager in the 1990s could go to an electronics store, buy a box of parts, and put together his own PC, then download a bootlegged copy of Apple's or

Microsoft's operating system and in a few hours have a fully functioning computer that was more powerful and reliable than the one I bought from IBM in the early 1990s for several thousand dollars that connected to the Internet, but which mine could not.

In some of the largest "advanced" economies it is not unusual to see expenditures on communicating-enabled computers consuming between 7 and 10 percent of a nation's expenditures. In Western Europe, people spend almost as much on their digital toys, devices, TV, social media, and smartphones as they do on groceries. The continuing innovation that had been so supported by governments in dozens of countries between the 1940s and the 1980s has now been superseded by the private sector, insuring that more changes will come from a larger collection of IT firms than in earlier decades.

Finally, the post-World War II restoration of open trade practices, combined with better and less expensive transportation and increased economic productivity, made it possible for people from multiple countries to meet and work with each other, creating shared expectations, tastes in music and food, and common practices. I could walk into an IBM sales office in any of over 100 countries and meet colleagues who did the exact same work as I, using the same systems, organizing their offices and organizations the same way, and who had the same kinds of customers that I had back in the United States. Their customers attended the same universities, read the same books, and did the same kind of work. It worked and the world got richer for it. Where it did not work, it got poorer, as occurred in the Soviet Union, China, and India, for example. People learned to speak English and to use computers the same way for the same purposes. They learned from each other. If I could not get my fancy mobile phone to work in Rome or Zurich, people helped me solve the problem in the same way as a neighbor in Madison, Wisconsin, and in English too. All of us were seemingly clutching Apple or Samsung phones. So, we can conclude that diffusion was facilitated by many hundreds of millions of people becoming more alike than different in certain ways, and one of those was in their use of information technologies.

Reflections on What Happened

Before moving on to other issues, pause for a moment to take in the speed and breadth of what just happened. In 1970, mainframes were locked up in large organizations; there were no PCs. In 1980, minicomputers could be seen on shop floors in factories and soon after tens of millions of desktop computers were popping up, most in the United States. By the end of the decade, there were millions of these. In the 1990s IBM sold over a quarter million "minis" (AS400s) and it was not the only vendor doing so in big quantities. In 1990 it was the rare person who had a laptop, by 2000 it seemed every businessperson did. Smartphones were still science fiction, so too smart watches and tablets. Cell phones (also called mobile phones) appeared in the 1990s, but remember they were portable "flip phones" that did not yet do computing. They looked more like miniature versions of my Honda car than high tech gadgets. Smartphones and tablets, which did, were twenty-first century innovations that now seems even the poorest people have.

It is a testimonial to the inherent flexibility of such general-purpose technologies that they could be shaped by different groups for new purposes. While the long-established camera manufacturers were selling film and cameras, Japanese consumer electronics producers with growing experience in making digital devices, such as better music systems, introduced digital cameras in the early 1990s. Kodak, which had developed photography's originally digital technology, ignored what was happening and so by the end of the decade the world's photographers had abandoned film and Kodak; the company's customers had gone digital. These same consumers had already acquired experience buying digital products before making this new decision, largely with microwave ovens then with personal computers. Similar tales could be told of non-computerized products becoming digital in industry, office work, and consumer goods. The obvious ones in many homes involved computer-managed consumption of electricity and fuel, and programmable TVs that could now display Internet-based video streaming.

It was no accident that old-line telephone companies had become major entertainment and movie behemoths by 2020. In the United States the iconic AT&T was seen as discouraging customers from continuing their use of POTS—Plain Old Telephone Service—which had been one of the great American technologies of the late nineteenth and all of the twentieth century. Most Americans under the age of 30 do not understand what the Great AT&T had been in the United States, others when asked if they had heard of IBM responded, "Huh? No." It happened to me and to many of my retired colleagues from IBM, yet this was a company that had employed some one million people and generated over a trillion dollars in revenue over the course of over a century. The times were changing, again.

If the history of computing is long enough that a room full of historians can speak of multiple arcs of development and inform their studies with more nuanced piles of evidence, they did not act alone. As our next chapter describes, computer users and society's observers, too, have been exposed to computing for two generations. Whole nations have now engaged repeatedly in discussions about the benefits and dangers of information and its underlying digital technologies. Their issues take up greater attention of the human race than do ruminations of historians. So, it is to the former's concerns to which we turn to next.

Chapter 3
Early Views of Computing

The public did not learn about the existence of computers until a year after the end of World War II and even then, initially just in the United States and largely if they read short pieces in the *New York Times*. Articles in the press began appearing in North America and Western Europe in the late 1940s, but they were few and far between. That changed in the 1950s as a more diverse set of newspapers, magazines and books describing this new technology began circulating on both sides of the Atlantic and in Japan. Engineers and government officials represented a tiny exception in that they were familiar with the technology, because they engaged in building them. Worldwide this group made up just a few thousand knowledgeable people scattered across Europe, North America, parts of Central and Eastern Europe, and Japan. That was all about to change.

By the end of the 1960s, large swaths of literate, usually urban dwelling, citizens in the industrialized world had heard about computers as large, fascinating, if little understood technology but magically wonderfully new devices. They were positioned as marvelous tools to assist in the creation of new eras, new ways of doing things. These new machines competed for their attention with the darker potential of nuclear weapons and the more hopeful prospects of space travel. Simultaneously in the late 1950s and increasingly in the 1960s and 1970s, commercial manufacturers of computers advertised their products in industry trade magazines, business and public sector press, and slowly on television. As the number of people who worked in data processing increased, they, too, began developing points of view about computing, sharing their perspectives with friends and family. (But not all; IBM spouses joked at their loved one's retirement parties how they had no idea what their breadwinners did at work!) With the dissemination of PCs starting in the late 1970s, the dam of opinions burst, flooding the world with opinions about computing that continued to flow rapidly through almost every country in the world through most age groups.

© Springer Nature Switzerland AG 2020
J. W. Cortada, *Living with Computers*,
https://doi.org/10.1007/978-3-030-34362-0_3

Early Reactions to Computers

Surveys, studies of advertising content, statistics on sales of books, and articles published on computing by all manner of media left a long trail of evidence documenting people's expanding knowledge. Several observations can be extracted from that massive experience. The first and most obvious is that awareness of the existence of computing and of its value to society evolved and diffused at about the same speed, as did the technology itself. Big mainframe computers locked behind glass and metal doors in building basements and secure sites in corporations did not lend themselves to shaping public opinion. There is nothing like ignorance to stimulate concerns, however, as Americans saw with the light comedy movie, *Desk Set* (1957) in which a computer-savvy consultant comes into a company to computerize (it used the word *automate*) research that threatened to put the corporate librarians out of a job (in the end it did not). The movie reflected a fear that automation (a term made popular in the early 1950s) would create massive ill-defined unemployment. Use of computers changed many jobs over the next half century, but also created many new ones. However, so few people understood that fact that fearing the end of work has remained a constant fear to the present. Periodically, journalists, even economists, and MIT professors threw fuel on that fear fire, but so far have been disproven—jobs were lost, many changed, and new ones created.

PCs and later laptops, mobile phones and smartphones exposed hundreds of millions of people to computing in short order—in one generation—from the halls of all manner of industrialized societies to some of the poorest villages in Africa, India and Southeast Asia where the demand for electricity was increasingly too, motivated by the need to recharge smartphones, and no longer solely by the desire to have light, power small machines, and to pump water.

Then and now people sheltered mixed, nuanced feelings about the technology; I discuss that more below. While ignorance of the specifics of the technology remained widespread for decades, that lack of understanding failed to dissuade people from being curious about what they could do, to stop worrying about the potential negative effects on jobs, or to fear their effects on the development of nuclear war weapons, Big Brother control over one's privacy, civil liberties, and ability to go about their lives. Laced through their mixed nervousness were positive and negative interests in what this technology was doing to society. Was it leading to the development of knowledge workers, an Information Society? What did that mean? Was its diffusion the culmination of the Scientific Age? Did it herald the end of religion and its supposed superstitions, as a new secular society emerged invigorated by massive bodies of data and ironclad disciplines of highly intelligent machines? Were machines and humans to merge into some singularity? That last discussion represents a discourse stimulated in part by the anticipation that computing—artificial intelligence—was now almost smart enough to take over many of humanity's functions. The smells of opportunities and fears whiffed through the air of modern society.

How Corporations Responded

Yet a third pattern of thinking unfolded slowly at nearly the same time, as evidence unfolded about what computers did to make the world a better place. Beginning largely with management in large corporations and government agencies, enterprises began collecting and using information less expensively, faster, and more accurately than before. In the case of businesses, that trend converted into declining operating costs, more profits, and new services and products. By the end of the 1980s evidence created by business professionals and business school professors had accumulated across dozens of industries that how organizations operated were changing, thanks to the greater use of computing. Users had gone through an initial phase in the 1950s–1970s of simply automating existing work processes.

It then became increasingly evident that users would need to go beyond that activity if they were to fully optimize use of this technology. To that end they began to change how they organized work to take advantage of their growing understanding of the capabilities of computers. Thus, for example, banks installed ATMs to let routine mundane retail transactions occur between customers and machines; later online banking after the arrival of the Internet. "Expert systems" combined with telephony allowed companies to begin answering questions their customers and employees had using software, thereby eliminating the need for so many workers in call centers, assigning them to other work within an enterprise or simply scooting them out the door. Mundane rule-based decision-making could be shifted to computers, beginning in the 1980s, such as whether to issue someone a credit card or authorize a car loan.

A dramatic change became evident on the floors of manufacturing facilities. They became cleaner, quieter, and safer for workers. An automotive manufacturing plant in the 1950s or 1960s was filled with workers doing repetitive physical tasks that led to back problems and other skeletal and muscular ills that prematurely aged them. Robots governed by computers began taking over that repetitive work, such as welding and screwing, while reducing worker exposure to paint fumes. The painter now sat at a keyboard apart from the vehicle, rather than personally spraying a car. Heavy objects moved about more efficiently and quickly, again reducing physical strain on employees.

The overall process for manufacturing a car changed, leading to an approach whereby instead of putting together one model of cars on a production line, a plant could assemble multiple ones on the same line, such as, say, three sedans, followed by several small pickup trucks, and then more cars, and so forth. Flexibility in responding to changing demand for vehicles became possible, indeed easier, although in practice factories tended to specialize in one or few models. The percent of workers who "bent metal" in such factories declined, while the total number employed often remained nearly as high as before, but now engaged in such other work as planning, supply chain management, and quality control—all jobs that were physically less demanding and safer, better paid, and intellectually more interesting and demanding, and required considerable reliance on computers.

This was particularly the case in factories that made computer chips and digital devices—a whole new set of jobs that did not exist prior to the arrival of the computer. The downside for those who worked in chip manufacturing, however, was that their great use of water often led to pollution of nearby groundwater supplies, a problem not recognized for many years after manufacturing of such products had begun. Their rates of cancer ticked up. So, all was not perfect.

An appetite for more information with which to conduct business and make decisions became evident by the end of the 1960s. By the end of the next decade for those working in offices the volume of desired data, indeed what they required, to go about their work had grown exponentially. People were educated at both the undergraduate and graduate levels to want and use more data. They learned to model alternative solutions, costs and benefits, using software to massage growing bodies of data, while the media used more computer generated statistics to go about its work. Photographs of offices in all types and sizes of businesses and organizations of the 1960s displayed rows of file cabinets; by the end of the 1980s, these had become scarce, while every desk seemed to have a terminal on it, and by the end of the 1990s, most a laptop or a PC. Today, we are led to believe workers in coffee shops. That, however, remains more myth than fact, but the trend is obvious—the ability to work anywhere at any time.

Of course, a naiveté crept in noticed by older workers who had learned their work before computers came along: younger employees took too literally what they saw on a screen. If a spreadsheet indicated that the answer to a question was "x" they tended to believe that because a computer had generated the answer, while the more experienced worker who had to develop the answer by hand in earlier times might be forgiven for more often questioning how the mathematics generated by the software to arrive at that answer when his or her tacit knowledge suggested an alternative one was more likely. Was a misplaced coma or poorly constructed formula proffering ten million when it made more sense for the answer to be closer to one million? It is not clear if today workers are more discriminating in what they believe pops up on a screen, given the acceptance as truth so much false (fake) news that appeared on websites all over the world since 2010. Computer literacy had evolved from just knowing how to do work on a machine to also include discriminating about the authenticity of what data appeared on a screen. Bill Aspray, a long-term student of how people use information, and I have been looking at this issue and our research suggests that a new digital literacy may be needed to teach people how to discriminate between accuracy and falsehoods. It is a mantra first voiced by advocates of how best to use statistics in the early twentieth century, then again when this branch of mathematics became fashionable for "the masses" during the Total Quality movement in the 1990s.

Sensors and the Hard Sciences Join Forces

Less visible, but easily as important has been the role of computers in operating sensors, collecting vast quantities of data that these technologies could organize into forms other computers could take action on, based on or that could be presented to humans for their study and use. Weather data is one of the most obvious earliest examples, dating to the 1950s. But computers have monitored almost every type of observation one could imagine about physical objects and activities. Changing sea levels, amount of pollutants in the ground and water and air are documented, monitored, and reported on for human mitigation. Even the humble traffic counters we bump over in our cars inform city officials about where they need more lights or lanes. Studying life forms, their atoms, and diseases improved using computers. Modeling alternatives in science, engineering, business and other human activities did too, because of the massive quantities of data sensors collect. It is why, for example, experts on climate change increase their levels of confidence about what the Earth's climate will look like by 2100. Economic forecasting has been a routine input into national government policies for the majority of the world's nations for over two decades, for OECD countries since the 1980s. The Soviet Union's senior leaders even wanted to run their entire economy using computers as early as the 1950s, but the technology was not sufficiently developed to accomplish that task. While the technology is still not ready to take it on, the appetite to do so continues to grow. The history of computing was always accompanied by massive doses of hubris, serving up great interest in doing more with the technology.

Society Debated the Role of Computers

The list of contributions made by users of computers increases as more is done. It has not always gone smoothly from one success to another, but in aggregate the positives outnumbered the negatives, so far. Each generation debated the role of computers and had their concerns, often driven either by the changing nature of the technology or the circumstances surrounding it. Fears of automation and job loss remained a constant, pollution and medical exposures too. There is little reason to believe that these dynamics will end. Two examples illustrate the issue, first the discussion France had about American computers in the shaping of an Information Age in the 1960s–1980s, and, second, the debate over privacy and social media on both sides of the Atlantic that bubbled up in the 2010s. Each is a cautionary tale of expectations, innocence about computers, and the importance of the technology as tools to shape an entire society's views and actions.

French companies and government agencies installed computers in the 1950s–1970s at rates comparable to other advanced economies, while France led the world in early use of intelligent phone services at home and office—its famed

Minitel system. Public debate about the influence of specifically IBM—seen as an American corporation even though it had a large French employee base in France—and of other U.S. firms in France in the 1960s and 1970s stimulated debates about their roles and that of French companies that were seen as under siege. In 1976, the national government commissioned a study of the impact of computing and tele-communications for the future of French society. From that study came new terms and concepts, most notably that of *telematics*, the idea of merged computing and telecommunications. What should have been a dry government report turned into both a "best seller" and the stimulus for a broad national discussion about the future of information in society. The haggling back and forth over ideas and with debates about the pros and cons of the American role mixed with what the French thought of their own digital future. This exercise helped shape national policies that encour-aged local (French, also other European) development of a computing industry beyond earlier initiatives. These failed in the face of the harsh realities of an already entrenched IBM and European-wide difficulty in mounting an effective challenge to other Americans firms, too. It did not help that the broader conversation entwined with anti-American discourse. Ultimately from a business perspective, it was a fail-ure of Europeans to scale up, the same issue we discussed earlier about British failures to thrive in the computer business.

Nonetheless, over the next few years the French debate spilled over into other West European countries. In France the public embraced a positive view of comput-ing—telematics—as harbinger of a better life. France and other nations sporting the most extensive experience with computers at work signed on to that positive future, despite concerns about the possibility of lost jobs, a greater angst across Western Europe than in France. While expressing in surveys a willingness to be retrained in better uses of computers, workers proved less willing to participate in the creation of a Brave New World. When the Internet became available, use of the older now less functional Minitel slowed adoption of the Internet until the end of the century. Overall, the French intellectually embraced the positives of computing with less critical scrutiny of its limitations. The exception to this generalization occurred within academic and professional circles where the greatest understanding of com-puting resided. But their nuanced views were muted. After the May days of 1968 Europe was entering a period of economic expansion, life was getting better.

The second case of debate and naiveté regarding computing's impact bubbled up in the 2010s in Western Europe first, but by early 2018 in the United States as well. In the U.S. it had become obvious that the Russians and President Donald Trump's presidential campaign of 2016 had disseminated much false information sufficient to cause his opponent to lose the presidential election.

West Europeans had a far greater concern about the role all manner of informa-tion handlers played when dealing with the personal information of individuals. The adoption of social media tools by the public at large in the early 2000s led the European Union (EU) and national regulators to explore how such enterprises as Facebook, Google, and Amazon handled information of individuals. They became concerned about the volume and variety of information collected, studied, and made available to other companies, notably to advertisers. The public became alarmed, too, which reinforced efforts by regulators to protect privacy of an individual's data. With revelations in the United States, and almost simultaneously in Europe of Russian dissemination of fake facts about candidates, of Facebook's sloppy permission for such fake sites and facts to circulate to its users, raised alarm bells in the U.S.

Like their European counterparts, American citizens became concerned and began demanding protections of their private data. The Trump Administration barely moved to assuage them. In the process, citizens on both sides of the Atlantic began to realize how naïve they had been in believing what they saw coming through their newsfeeds and Facebook accounts. Demands for regulation increased, while critics suggested that people stop using Facebook and curate more carefully their Google queries. The happy-go-lucky acceptance of how wonderful smartphones had made their lives now came into question. It is too early to tell if the anti-computer sentiment will grow, but what is more certain from surveys conducted by such organizations as the Pew Foundation and Gallop is that Americans were beginning to see that computing had both positive and negative features, that while IT could be a force for good, old concerns about state surveillance and agnostic decision-making by artificial intelligence had become worrisome. People around the world were concerned as well, coming to a more knowledgeable understanding of how computing affected their private lives, work, and even the construct of their societies.

Management's Evolving Views

Managers have made most of the decisions to acquire computers and how best to deploy them over the past seven decades. The one notable exception to this behavior concerns such consumer electronic products as PCs, tablets, laptops, and smartphones used by individuals for their personal activities. In the twenty-first century, private retail expenditures roughly equaled that of organizations in most countries; in the prior century, organizations made a larger percent of the decisions about what to acquire. So, management's views shaped profoundly human views of computing for over a half century and still do today. Until the second half of the 1980s, the center of activity involving computers and, therefore, the center of where thinking about this technology rested overwhelmingly in large organizations using mainframe computers and within the companies that supplied them with these technologies.

They collectively fixated on technological evolutions in the 1950s and 1960s, which were occurring so fast that their collective data processing ecosystem was constantly trying to understand its economic and operational implications. Everyone seemed focused on trying to understand trends and forecasts. By the mid-1960s growing consensus held that hardware would continue to become more reliable and keep running, that computer power would continue to increase, so too improved cost performance of computer storage; that the same would apply to all peripheral equipment, including terminals; and that telecommunications would become faster, better, and incorporate more functions. Users and their managers were told that overall hardware costs would increase (because they were acquiring so much more of it), but their expense would decrease as percent of total IT budgets (hardware, software, personnel, services). Managers, technologists, and computer vendors anticipated spectacular positive developments in software, such as shorter times required to write new programs, using easier-to-use programming languages that were more like human languages; that the cost of software would increase as a percent of an IT department's total budget; that their functions would be better and easier, while the cost of maintaining their programs would decline. Databases would come into their own as new methods and tools for organizing ever-increasing amounts of data.

For the most part, these forecasts came about, transforming into multi-decade descriptions of trends. The number of technically capable people increased, making it easier for companies to embrace computers. While increasing one's reliance, computers did not become easier to run, so by necessity the number of people who could operate these grew. Feeding these machines with increasing amounts of new software did too. In the United States there were an estimated 10,000 programmers in 1955, in 1985 that number had climbed to 330,000, while the nation went from 1000 computers to 1.1 million (including PCs). Similar patterns were evident in other industrialized economies.

Everyone seemed to be encouraged to recognize that data processing technology was a useful tool; that for what computers were used for should be chosen carefully (which is where vendors could offer assistance); that companies should experiment with new technology; and that enterprises and governments would suffer the costs of "lost" opportunities should they hesitate to embrace computing. It was a conversation about optimizing use of all this new technology. It had become an Age of Hubris. What happened? The first generation experimented and learned. It focused on goals, planning, developing the rationale for applications of computing, finding ways to use traditional cost justification methods applied to hardware and software, shaping data processing budgets, then controlling them. Early users worked out how they should interact with computers, sales personnel, and other technical staffs.

By the mid-1980s much of that preliminary work had been done. Many IT organizations devoted much attention to tracking how many computers they had, what they were being used for, and in finding new uses for these. Next, PCs had to be connected to mainframes in massive networks, while every department seemed to want their own machines and so had to go through a condensed version of what first generation data processing personnel had to in order to figure out what to do and why. By the early 1980s many also feared the worst—a disaster, such as a flooded data center, loss of electrical power, malfunctioning hardware or software. Large organizations had become so dependent on computers that there could be no turning back, so it seemed everyone began developing backup plans to keep their computers operating.

At the same time management perched at the top of corporations and governments could no longer leave computing to middle and lower managers or to technical staffs and computer vendors, consultants, and academics. Too much was at stake, too much data was now in machine-readable form. Harvard Business School professors, computer scientists, and IBM executives were telling the world that information was a "corporate asset," an "investment" and no longer simply a cost. Now they had to invest in "enabling technologies" to unlock the value of their data and to do that they had to face the "challenge of ignorance." Valuing computing and its uses continued as a relentless, yet essentially, positive exercise in the 1980s, as organizations deployed computers in offices, automated work in manufacturing and processing plants, and in training workers. By then millions of people were using computers at work and increasingly with their PCs at play and in private life. The world of work has finally become entwined with computing. Let's see by how much.

Work Changed Because of Computers

Historians would later conclude that all this work, while done enthusiastically and often with a positive attitude, was not always well done, with considerable guessing, fumbling, and bumbling along the way. Management learned that many of the issues involving data processing were less about computers and more about traditional business issues: budgeting, personnel, making and selling goods, and measuring financial results.

One sticking problem before the early 2000s was how to measure results, specifically costs and productivity, return on investments compared to money spent on other machines. Another concerned how best to deploy computers (i.e., in centralized data centers or distributed out into offices and plants). Embedded in all of those operational concerns was the growing realization that the technology was just not going to stabilize; it kept changing and changing. Standalone computers became networked systems, smaller ones even tinier, yet all the while with greater functions and memories to store and swizzle information. The conversation shifted to the nature of all these changes. By the mid-1990s, it had become clear that the features of technologies were themselves also changing the nature of work, raising questions about what people actually did at their desks while staring at their terminals or PCs. Questions and uncertainties pervaded conversations about what these all meant, how people were responding, what could be expected of them. Nor was outdoor work immune. Someone checking on a natural gas leak in the 1980s dug a ditch to find a rupture in a pipe, while in the 1990s they dropped a sensor down a hole connected to a laptop perched on the hood of a pickup truck to literally "sniff" for a leak, which could then be plugged with a substance that reminded older workers of chewing gum used to fix a radiator hose leak in an Army Jeep. Computerized sensors soon made their way into their world, along with satellites reading all manner of outdoor meters from space, including home electricity meters. Building contractors viewed blueprints on their laptops while carpenters ordered materials using both their mobile phones and from a list of materials an architect had created online and had emailed to construction workers.

People were told to go beyond notions of information as a corporate asset to now managing knowledge so that it could be "leveraged," while viewing work as processes (work steps and their computing), to "reengineer" them for efficiency. That last initiative resulted in significant numbers of lost jobs as firms optimized and streamlined processes in the 1990s and early 2000s. The dark concerns of workers of the 1950s were back, but this time they remained. Viewing the movie *Desk Set* now felt eerily contemporary, again.

By the dawn of the new century the digital experts had become a global community of millions of technologists, IT experts, and aficionados. Most senior executives had experienced managing the introduction of a big computer system or application in their organizations, and hundreds of millions of employees knew how to work using terminals and PCs, many millions how to write software. How people managed in a world filled with computers changed. They thought in terms of processes, not just jobs or tasks. They saw computers as libraries of information. They began linking their organizations to those of customers, suppliers, and competitors using the Internet and private networks. They automated, used expert systems, and recognized the uncomfortable reality that computing involved an endless round of "waves of change." They thought in terms of "supply" and "value" chains, business lingo for how one interacted on a regular basis, say, from the point when a diamond was mined out of the ground until halfway around the world a young man slipped an engagement ring onto the finger of his true love, with businesses understanding every step of the way and who and what organizations should do the required work. And of course, all this had to be done in a faster and timelier manner. The redesign of work involved eliminating work steps, automating others, and outsourcing some to more efficient enterprises. Computers made it possible to choreograph the transformed world. Humankind had become more interconnected.

By 2010 one could describe an organization as an information ecosystem, with computing serving as the digital plumbing in the enterprise, because every function in a corporation now used computerized data linked to every other part of the firm or agency. All were dependent on using computing to deal with each other. Computing and its data were recognized as the glue that held together an organization, even its information ecosystem and industry. There was no escape, as IT was today's permanent reality.

Some Lessons to Consider

Lessons of history could finally be drawn upon to teach managers about how computers spread around the world, how governments and large enterprises leveraged IT to improve entire national economies and global enterprises, not to mention small firms. Old issues lingered, because the technologies kept changing: how to select what to use and for what, how to cost justify them and measure the return on their expense, how to measure risk of failure and potential benefits of success, and how to define who best should do the work. The list of things to keep up with was as long as ever, feeding management's chronic nervousness about these ongoing changes in computing's forms and functions constant. The Internet forced more intimate collaboration and dependencies on suppliers and customers, among others. One important recent shift that occurred was to greater dependency on computerized analytics, cloud computing (computing outside one's enterprise, hence possibly giving up some direct control over it), ubiquitous sensors, and split second continuous data collection. Career planning became more challenging for many as they saw a generation of middle managers eliminated, since computers could now move information up and down the enterprise without human handlers, while loyalty to an employer eroded as layoffs and turnovers increased. Meanwhile, a billion more people entered the middle class and they were now buying PCs and smartphones. The world of the digital community had expanded, democratized, and it seemed everyone had an opinion about it.

Chapter 4
How People View Computing Today

Since humans now have considerable experience with many types of computing they have opinions about this technology, ranging from their importance and practicality to their degree of effectiveness, benefits, and use. As we sit here at the end of the second decade of the new century, summarizing world views is difficult to do and the future even more improbable to forecast. But a snapshot in time is better than none. Survey data show that people around the world hold nuanced views of the technology's role. For sake of simplicity we can divide them into two communities: the general public and those that use/work with/promote/have a stake in the use of IT, from academics to computer scientists and professionals, to CEOs of IT companies. Let's begin with the public at large and what it thinks.

What the Public Thinks in "Emerging" Economies

Much of what the public in developed economies said about computers is reflected in our previous discussion, so to see if there are other differing or fresh perspectives a peak at what people think in emerging economies makes sense. For one thing, they rely more on smartphones and the Internet for a majority of their interactions with computing than in more developed economies where use of PCs remains quite high too—the three sets of technologies that experts on IT and related topics generally agree will play greater roles in the future of the planet, especially smartphones.

For another, emerging economies are producing the next billion people and have the youngest populations in the world, which means in aggregate they will probably be the longest living users of IT in our current century. Besides, they are now the fastest adopters of computing of all kinds, catching up to those folks who lived in more developed economies that have been accumulating IT for longer periods of time. The new entrants into a more digital world will increasingly influence humanity's experience with computing.

© Springer Nature Switzerland AG 2020
J. W. Cortada, *Living with Computers*,
https://doi.org/10.1007/978-3-030-34362-0_4

Their countries today include Colombia, India, Jordan, Kenya, Lebanon, Mexico, Philippines, South and Central Africa, Tunisia, Venezuela, and Vietnam among others, not to mention over four dozen in Africa. Additionally about two thirds of China (some 700 + million people) would fit into such a list, but there is too little survey evidence to understand fully what those Chinese think. The other third reflect much of the behavior of advanced economies: heavy reliance on mobile computing, social media, and so forth. Emerging economies are located mostly in Africa, Southeast Asia, all over Latin America, and large swaths of the Middle East. Demographers are in general agreement that each of these areas will experience significant growth in populations during most of the rest of this century before tapering off, a growth spurt that will far exceed that of the most advanced economies. At the same time, population growth has already begun to level off on both sides of the Atlantic, among today's most intensive users of computing.

We can pay attention to their views because so many now already use these technologies. So what are their *bono fides*? Worldwide people adopted mobile computing rapidly. In barely the first 12 years of the existence of smartphones in the most advanced economies between 70% and 95% of the adult population used them. In emerging economies, adoption proved a bit slower, because of the relative high cost of such tools, but even there adoption proved extensive. In India, for example, a quarter used smartphones and another 40% mobile phones. The median populations in developing economies used both: about 45% smartphones, a third mobile phones. Put another way, only about 6% of adults in developed countries did not use either smartphones or mobile phones, 17% in developing countries. Moreover, adoption of mobile phones began early in the new century, while smartphones only became available worldwide after 2007. In advanced economies by 2018, some 90% of adults used the Internet in one way or another. Digital connectivity and use of the Internet in developing economies ranged from a low of roughly 35% to a high of over 50%. In other words, the world was largely wired and had been for a while.

So, what are residents in developing economies saying, particularly about mobile computing and connectivity to the greater Internet? First, adults report that the vast majority have access or use these technologies today; hence are both reliant upon them and understand some of the implications of their use. They are referring to smartphones and the Internet, less so any other type of computing. They use social media apps, specifically Facebook and WhatsApp, although the other nearly half dozen major social media tools are in wide use as well. The Pew Research Center reported in 2019 that over 90% of smartphone users also relied on social media software. Just 10% less used social media tools with other forms of computing. The vast majority celebrates their ability of staying in touch with friends, family and work associates using smartphones, but also valued these tools for obtaining news and weather reports. *The Economist* reported that their favorite uses involved applications in support of friendships, connecting to family, and all manner of fun and entertainment.

In fact, around the world, people who use a combination smartphones and social media are routinely exposed to people of different backgrounds and to a larger array of friends they normally would not otherwise communicate with. These users also access more facts about health and local government services. Their interactions are more frequent than non-users with people of different religions, socio-economic status, and who hold differing political views. This data offers potential evidence that increasing numbers of people may become more tolerant of differing perspectives, a conclusion that if it plays out, would fly in the face of all the media accounts of racial, nationalist, and gender frictions all over the world. Time will tell.

But, as with many other things in life, software presents positive and negative experiences, such as Facebook. As in the most industrialized economies, the majority of adults worry about the negative effects of computing on children, because the little ones could be exposed to immoral content, harmful material, or false information. In fact, some two-thirds think mobile phones have posed a negative influence on children. Yet, the more developed an economy is the more residents believe they must have access to such technologies to go about their lives. The converse is true in an opposite way: the less developed an economy the less they need access to such tools. Much as in wealthier societies, people wax eloquently about the benefits of such technologies for themselves personally, but less so for society at large. Nearly half, to be specific, believe that social media has been harmful to society, as compared to smartphones, which some two-thirds believe has been good for society as a whole. As with parents in the United States and in many parts of Europe, parents are curtailing the amount of screen time their children have and curate what they see. Eight out of ten people share these views worldwide and already half are implementing constraints on their children's access to these.

Adults believe that mobile computing frees up their time and improves their productivity, although a minority in most countries acknowledges they waste time using their smartphones. The older a user is, the more likely they are to believe these technologies save time, while many under the age of 30 say these technologies encourage unproductive uses. The more educated a user is, the more likely they are to believe that mobile computing is productive. Threaded through their perspectives worldwide is concern about negative impact on the health of children who, if they spend too much time playing with such devices, do not get enough physical exercise, do not develop social skills needed to interact with other people, are potentially exposed to radiation and, if rumors are to be believed, to seizures. Their beliefs align neatly with concerns of people living on both sides of the Atlantic. As in the West, the better educated one is, the more likely they are to own such devices. Only about a third of people in such societies own a PC or tablet.

As they gained experience with computing, people worldwide expressed growing concerns about the downsides of mobile computing. Concerns about privacy in the West, use of Facebook and other social media platforms by the Russians to influence the results of American presidential elections, Chinese censorship of what its citizens could obtain over the Internet, similar actions across the Middle East, the spread of rumors and false facts that led to riots, acts of violence, and increased hateful language were all appearing as concerns around the world. Residents in developing countries now have as much experience in such matters as folks in the rest of the world.

While over 8 in 10 believe computing kept them more informed about current events, just over 7 in 10 believe the technology makes it easier to manipulate people's opinions using false information and in spreading rumors. While social media tools have equipped people with the ability to voice their political points of view, and thus participate in their local political processes, between 65% and nearly 70% feel that local politicians using these tools could manipulate them. Only half think such tools can bring diverse people together, while just slightly more believe the combination of mobile phones of all types (not just smartphones), social media, and use of the Internet create greater divisions in political opinions in their countries. In other words, as in the United States and in evidence in the 2019 European Union elections, political divisions were increasing and growing numbers of people thought computing facilitated those divides.

Overall worldwide, more than three-quarters of the population believes computing is keeping them up-to-date, informed about topics relevant to them, and focused on issues significant to them. Worldwide people report that false and negative content is presented to them on a regular basis, through computing. While historians are just now beginning to study the existence and use of fake facts and misinformation, it is clearly evident to hundreds of millions of people that these exist and that they need to be wary of them.

The magic of computers is gone, replaced with a realistic view of the technology based on experience. That transition in how the world views computing cannot be underestimated. It took essentially 75 years for that to happen, and there is no turning back. While the technology will continue to change—and the world's population understands that—all these people are more focused on its uses, rather than on the magic of its bells and whistles.

What IT Gurus Think

Returning briefly to studies by the Pew Research Center suggests how experts on the technology view humankind's overall experience with IT. This organization has surveyed such individuals for two decades. Over one thousand experts participated just since 2017–2018. These include academics, business leaders, futurists, sociologists, experts involved in the operation and governance of the Internet, others working in think tanks, sociologists, public officials, and so forth. Their observations and anecdotes can be quickly summarized.

As people in general around the world do, they view "digital life" as a concoction of positives and negatives. On the plus side they admired the ability of people to connect to each other the most in human history, thanks to the availability of the Internet. Digital tools made it possible to invent, redesign, and innovate across all manner of human activities, including people's lives and careers, to find better more fulfilling jobs, and to meet new people. Individuals could now share information that assisted others and improved safety, such as about medical practices, pointing out resources for medical assistance, and warn about criminal activity, even about traffic congestion. Perhaps the most publicized positive discussed almost from the dawn of the World Wide Web has been the efficiency with which business transactions could be conducted. We have only to think about eBay and Amazon in the West and Alibaba Group in China to get the idea. The Internet made it possible to change substantially how one acquired or moved goods and services, or experienced events. Finding the best options for any decision or action, connecting to relevant information in rapid fashion, and across all manner of human activity was seen as a distinct, dramatic, positive for online digital life.

But these experts had learned that not all aspects of the digital proved positive. On the negative side were equal numbers of problems and limitations. Having access all the time to everything involving human activities was seen as creating stress, anxiety, an impatience with people and organizations, while diminishing the face-to-face social contacts that had so characterized human interactions for hundreds of centuries. The image of a family of four sitting in a restaurant with each staring at their smartphone became an iconic meme of our time. The experts call that out as a problem. They also think people become addictive to specific products, stimulates heightened levels of emotional attachment to objects and points of view, such as around politics, leading to both political and social polarization. In business, they rightfully noted that employees increasingly have to be accessible 24/7 every day of the year. The days of going home after 8 h of work seemed under siege. As a result of these transformations tensions and mistrust were increasing worldwide. Such developments encourage concerns about security, privacy, and surveillance—three issues that came to dominate much of the discourse about modern digital life in most countries after 2010, and especially as Facebook, Google, Amazon and other Internet-born enterprises were criticized for their data management practices.

A third problem concerns "personal identity issues," by which they mean changing behaviors that were intensifying to shape one's image (a narcissist behavior perhaps), while linking to others through click-bating, liking, trolling, and pressuring others to conform to specific points-of-view. Some of the experts were reporting that in the process of participating in a digital world individuals were experiencing declining self-confidence and self-esteem, mistrusting others, and were assuming more negative views on all manner of subjects.

A fourth area experts characterized as negative concerns their perception that people are less focused today, by which they mean individuals do not dig as deeply into information as in the past—they use the term *shallow* to describe how people seek out and use facts, passing through much data but not pausing to reflect on its significance. They see people concentrating less time and focus on a particular task, of spending less time doing focused thinking. People want the "elevator answer," rather than to do the deep dive on a topic that might require, say, an hour-long lecture to explain an issue or to read a 500-page book on one topic. In today's language, they would prefer that you "net it out," or to use an old consultant's trope, when asked what time it is, people want the time, not a lecture on how time is calculated by a watch.

The pluses and minuses identified by those familiar with today's computing that they link to behaviors and consequences appeared within one generation. Such issues were rarely of concern before the wide accessibility of the Internet. Already they could see that the techno-enthusiasts of the 1950s–1990s were too exuberant. Today's experts offer caution, calling for prudence as humans engage with computing.

What Business and Government Leaders Think

But, what are those engaged with computing in organizations and enterprises talking about? What are the leaders of large companies investing in and worrying about? Hubris today, as over the past seven decades, continues to characterize many conversations about computing.

At the risk of over-simplifying matters, we engage in two short exercises to hint at what is happening. Each is suggestive of issues, both are not rigorous scientific surveys, yet are offered with the excuse that with the technology still churning and transforming no thorough analysis of these issues would add much to our understanding of human/computer relations, as they would likely become too dated sooner than we would want. So treat this as a snapshot in time. The first exercise involves cataloging topics business professionals are discussing on LinkedIn, the professional website that is almost like Facebook but for business people. I will use my personal LinkedIn account, because it includes nearly 1000 IT and business professionals; the second is listing the topics of articles that appeared in the IEEE Computer Society's lead magazine, *Computer,* which is written by and for computer scientists and IT technical experts. It is for many experts on computing, a "journal of record," meaning *the*, or key, authoritative place for information about trends in computing. In both cases, I extracted my findings at the same time Pew reported its findings from its 1000 experts.

After examining 2000 entries from LinkedIn, several observations jumped out. Everyone posting these entries was involved in developing, using, promoting, and experiencing the consequences of IT in their workplaces. They were engaged in the arena of today's institutional uses of information. They came from private and public sectors, universities, the United States, Western Europe, and Asia. Business people wrote the overwhelming majority of these entries. Second, over half discussed how best to deploy a particular technology or form of computing across functional areas, such as finance, logistics and marketing, or in specific industries, notably finance, banking, manufacturing, and automotive. Third, some 75% of the types of computing involved hybrid cloud, artificial intelligence, robotics, automation, often these various technologies in combination, such as AI and robotics, and for injecting innovation into an enterprise.

Soft issues were much discussed, most notably personal leadership as part of discussions of specific technologies. Almost all the advice on leadership came from managers and executives who had direct personal experience with computing, notably executives in software, hardware, and consulting/IT services firms. Less than a quarter felt they had to explain what a particular technology was, such as blockchain or hybrid computing (something they did repeatedly and more frequently 2–3 years earlier); they spent more time reporting on "best practices" in their implementations. Other topics included wearable computers in the workplace, data analytics, risk governance at the corporate board level once a company was highly dependent on the use of computers, role of virtual reality in the workplace, scaling businesses through use of IT (a favorite topic for over a decade), drones in business, science and national disasters, growing use of IT and AI in health and in the pharmaceutical industry worldwide, machine learning (a primitive form of AI now becoming dramatically more sophisticated), and the impact of computing on one's corporate culture. One surprising topic involved several contributors talking about the benefits of taking notes by hand in meetings rather than by using one's laptop, arguing the case that handwritten notes were better and that the note taker remembered details more thoroughly.

These presentations were overwhelmingly positive in tone. Comments made in response to these ranged all over the place from complimenting and confirming the findings presented by the original contributor to a few cautionary critiques almost designed to manage expectations, but without going negative or snarky as one see constantly on social media sites. Knowing many of the authors of original postings, I concluded that they chose their language carefully, so too the respondents, while the vast majority favored using emerging technologies, but understanding that there were best ways to do so.

So what did the more hardcore computer science community discuss? The authors came from around the world. They ranged from computer scientists at academic institutions to others who worked in the information processing industry, or were users of computing. The latter often had decades of experience and deep technical knowledge. All, too, entered the arena, working with both existing and emerging technologies, many actually creating them, so they were able to report on their progress and provide examples of their work. The Computer Society publishes monthly *Computer* with each issue presenting a half dozen, or more, articles. Each issue focuses on one broad theme. In 2018 these themes included software engineering, use of software in the health industry, two issues devoted to the nuts-and-bolts of cyber security, one each on the future of artificial intelligence, role of government regulators in the age of big data, and trends and forecasts (an annual feature published in January). Many of these themes carried over from earlier years and continued into 2019 when, for example, it devoted entire issues to cognitive computing systems, training of future cyber security experts, best practices in software protections, more about computing and healthcare, and a series of articles about software systems, their complexity, role of algorithms, and regulators. In short, while topics were highly technical in nature, they paralleled much of what one could see in LinkedIn, where the emphasis focused more on implementation and results regarding the kinds of technologies being developed by the authors in *Computer*.

There appeared to be a rough consensus about what issues on which to focus. For decades such approximately similar agendas existed in the broader world of institutional computing. As individual users became involved with computers, beginning largely in the 1980s, attempts to codify consensus issues by the professionals and amateurs also took place, often reflected in widely distributed magazines, concentrating on PCs. Because the technology facilitated sharing of information about all manner of computing, it should be of no surprise that interested parties would know what others were focusing on and be influenced by that collective group think.

There is growing pressure on providers of Internet services, phone services and social media coming from their customers to improve services. Citizens around the world are increasingly also demanding—no longer asking—that everyone have access to reliable Internet services. It is the same demand that people made over the past century for clean water and ubiquitous supply of reliable electricity. Users/citizens believe it is the responsibility of business providers and governments to create the infrastructure and make it easy to get into. The only debate seems to be whether it is a top priority or not, that varies by country but not the demand for access. Surveys demonstrating this attitude simply add evidence that information technologies are almost as important infrastructures for quality human life today as education, water, personal safety, and sanitation were to earlier generations.

Making Sense of the Wizards

What are we to make of these various views from citizens of the world, experts, and professional users and employees? What are they telling us about the influence and effects of computing on humankind? There are several messages that we can mine from their views and behaviors.

First, perhaps even foremost, people in most walks of life, social and economic positions, and their societies have, *so far*, bolted computing onto their own core activities in all its forms as assists. Others might argue *au contraire*, citing how work changed, how teenagers were heads down on screens, and so forth. But they would be wrong, because what people did had not changed fundamentally. They still went to work; still played games; still interacted with friends, neighbors, governments and family; still researched information useful to them, notably the price and availability of goods and services and weather reports; and still read materials that gave meaning to their lives. My own research on how Americans used information over the past two centuries confirms that reality; they essentially digitized and sped up accessibility to what they had relied on in the past. Now they could do that cheaper, faster, and have more of it. But the essential human acts had not yet changed. Their behavior is evident worldwide.

Second, humans are tool using creatures, and have been so for over a million years. As a species they know how to use tools, and perhaps most important, for what purposes. Every craftsman tells his or her children and apprentices that having the right tool makes all the difference in completing tasks in a proper manner. They know not to sweep up leaves in their backyard with a broom, rather to use a specially designed rake for the task. Using the butt end of a screwdriver to pound in a nail is not as effective as a hammer. Historians of computing and experts on the redesign of work processes confirmed that the discriminating understanding of how and when to use computing optimizes the use of this general-purpose technology has been a constant focus of users since the earliest computers. The debate continues today: When and how should we use artificial intelligence? What are the most effective forms of cloud computing, when, and where? How should we use the Internet to educate children? The list of questions is endless, but everyone's focus is singular: matching the tool to the task and computing is seen as a tool. While our tools are becoming more "intelligent," thanks to the application of AI functions, and while a few people are fearful that computers will take over the world (the fear of the singularity), not so today billions of people. They speak about apps, smartphones, the Internet, and Facebook much the same way as they do about cars, kitchen knives, and TV sets—as tools with which to do what they otherwise would have done in the absence of computing—work and entertainment.

I have long hammered hard on this point, informed by many years of observing the activities of such industries as automotive and banking, and my own employer, IBM. Both industries and IBM existed for the same purposes, providing at their core the same services for well over a century. Henry Ford made automobiles before World War I; today his company still assembles automobiles, even in many of the same cities as in earlier times. Ford Motor Company uses production lines, automation and computers, but it still makes vehicles. Banks still store our money, letting us draw it out of our accounts, and loans us funds for home mortgages, to buy automobiles, and to pay debts; these institutions also use computers. For over 130 years IBM has been about selling data processing tools to help all manner of organizations collect, store, analyze, and process information (data). It, too, uses computers, still has salesmen and data centers where people can process data (today using cloud computing), often using the same business and sales techniques it did a century ago.

Largely since the availability of the PC and Internet for the public at large, a parallel set of uses of these technologies came into their own: personal uses of IT, already mentioned both worth memorializing here. Since the invention of portable music systems, such as transistor radios in the 1950s, individuals have been using various forms of computing technologies to do what they had done for a long time before the arrival of computers. They listened to music on phonograph players before World War I, now they stream music to their smartphones. They watched television since the late 1940s, now they stream programs to their iPads, PCs, laptops, and smartphones. They do the same with movies, a form of entertainment they have enjoyed since the 1890s. People used every form of communications and media to keep up with news and sports: newspapers, telegraph, radio, TV, and now all manner of tools and forms connected to the Internet. When email became available in the 1980s they began communicating with friends and family as much as they did with colleagues at work. By the end of the 1990s they had figured out how to send photographs of picnics, family events, children, and other non-work related images to friends and relatives. Pursuing hobbies became a major incentive for using all manner of computing, particularly PCs, beginning in the late 1970s.

Two words we can use to describe these various uses of digital tools are *fun* and *entertainment*. People spend as much on IT in pursuit of these activities worldwide as do firms, governments, and educational institutions to do work. This should be of no surprise because individuals massively outnumber organizations and when they are not working they are having fun, being entertained, or going about their household chores and responsibilities. As at work, they reach out for the right tools to get these things done. It is a well-established pattern. In the United States in the 1800s as public libraries opened up all over the nation librarians complained that people were checking out more novels than they were history books or others that would allow one to learn a trade. Early TV proponents hoped it would become an educational tool and on both sides of the Atlantic whole countries tried to deliver instructions that way; they failed. People wanted comedy, movies, sports, weather, some news, and concerts. So, as we think through the relationship between computing and people, we should keep in mind that the two interact continuously across the entire spectrum of human activity in ways that predate the arrive of the computer.

Third, humans like to simultaneously use combinations of tools. That makes it possible to use the right tool for the right job. It also gives them the perspective needed to understand the strengths and limits of a specific tool. It is why, for example, parents love smartphones and the Internet for bringing them information and for communicating with other people, but are concerned that these may not be the most *effective* tools for educating and raising their children. It is why adults love the interaction of their involvement in political affairs, but increasingly worry that malicious data is being fostered on them. Put another way, they are learning that using the butt end of a screwdriver instead of a hammer to pound a nail into a piece of wood could lead to a slip in the ponding, increasing the odds of the screwdriver crashing into their other hand, but that same screwdriver is the perfect and safe tool for inserting a screw into a piece of wood.

Harking back to the idea that people use multiple tools reveals several important observations about computing. Look at the collection of tools one has in their home or at work and you see a variety that transcends time. Hammers have been around since the dawn of civilization, screwdrivers in their modern forms for over one century. But next to these you might see an electric nail gun that propels nails into wood using compressed air and electricity, while next to it might be a battery operated combination drill and screwdriver. In a kitchen we can see a gas operated stove/oven and an electric microwave oven. The former was developed in the nineteenth century, the later introduced long after World War II. Hand operated hedge clippers have been around for many centuries, and many home owners possess these elongated scissors, yet in the Western world probably also electric hedge clippers. The point is that people add to their tool kits more often than they discard old tools, providing that the tasks are the same from one period to another. People still need to pound on nails, screw things together, and trim shrubs. The list is quite endless. Yet, at the same time new tools make new tasks possible, too.

The same practices apply to information handling. People read paper books and e-books. They read newspapers and news online. They watch television and stream television programs through their smartphones, tablets, laptops, and PCs. They write condolence notes on paper, email correspondence, scan or physically mail documents or photographs, and simultaneously clutter their spaces with books, digital device, magazines, pencils, pens, pads of paper, notebooks and electronic notebook functions on their devices, keep an analog electric clock hanging in their kitchen, perhaps in the hallway (if fortunate enough) a manually wound Grandfather Clock, and check its accuracy by glancing at their digital smart watch made by Apple. You still need to read a paper map if hiking in most national parks around the world, but can use a GPS-based tool to be instructed on how to drive through Normandy, France or in downtown Chicago. In short, people accumulate multiple generations of information handling tools as they do other non-information handling ones, such as hammers and nail guns.

This behavior exists at work and at home. Walk into a large enterprise anywhere in the world and you will see a combination of new and old information handling tools in use simultaneously. It is not uncommon, for example, to still have to fill out paper forms, such as an application for a passport in many countries or to sign paper contracts, while other transactions in the same organization are conducted completely online. A tiny handheld calculator can often be found in someone's desk drawer, while online forms often calculate numeric results, such as online tax filing forms in the United States. File cabinets have not completely gone away, nor have copiers in an age of scanned digital documents. Enter a large office supply store and you will quickly see that over 25% of the products offered for sale are made out of paper, cardboard, or wood. All are for storing and preserving information. Writing instruments diversified from pencils and ink pens of the nineteenth century to ballpoint pens of the post-World War II to felt tip pens and other markers since the 1970s; all are still used today. Dear reader you still use pencils and paper, admit it, while your smartphone is parked inches away from you. Chalk and blackboards (white boards increasingly with felt tip pens) are still used in universities around the world that pride themselves on their engineering and computer science programs. It is a worldwide circumstance that people use old and new tools, analog and digital means of handling information.

People have long lived in an Information Age of some sort. Their increased dependence on ever-larger amounts of information represents the long-term general trend stretching across thousands of years. Sensationalist writers and reporters are correct when they proclaim such thoughts as more data is collected in 1 min around the world today than, say, in a decade or century in the past; that we have more information in our smartphone than if printed out would fit in the back of a truck, and so forth. They would be right. More interesting, such clever statements will be even more the case in the future as sensors continue to be implanted in all manner of human-made devices, our natural world, and in Space. The old will continue to mix with the new, as we are reminded every time NASA shows the world images of distant stars and planets taken by satellite-based cameras launched into Space one or more decades ago just now arriving close enough to take photographs.

Is There More to This Story?

Thinking of computers as the latest new tools and arguing that people are treating them as the most current hammer and screwdriver is, however, an insufficient perspective. While essentially correct, there is more to the story of computers. In our era in human history—the post-World War I period—scientific and technological innovations came so fast in such quantity that it is difficult to imagine people taking it all in to the extent that they could in earlier eras when they had centuries to do so. Historians have long documented the legal, social, cultural, political, and economic consequences of new technologies and innovations, such as the development of the stirrup and saddle, application of gun powder to cannon and rifles, much later various chemicals in the eighteenth and nineteenth centuries, the emergence of chemistry, physics and mathematics as central sources of new knowledge, electricity applied to work and home life, flight, and for a while the emergence of nuclear power.

Students of human behavior are debating the impact of screen time on young children with no scientific consensus yet achieved; as late as the 1990s economists were still pondering the economic impact of computers even though corporations had already voted with their budgets that these were useful tools. Hubris over the wonders of computing flooded into all corners of our lives. Experts could almost set their watches by when a new innovation would become reality from when the marketing professionals, pro-technological commentators, and magazine editors began cranking up their hubris machines—usually 4–5 years. Today, we hear that AI will momentarily do miracles and as I was writing the original draft of this chapter in 2019 that same week an IBM executive was quoted in the press as saying that within 3–5 years commercial versions of quantum computing would be available. As of 2019 it was still a highly experimental technology little understood outside of computer science research centers, let alone taken seriously by corporations already invested in massive uses of existing parallel computing and the old Von Neumann Architecture. History had taught users not to embrace new technologies without confidence that they would work at least as well—and as safely—as what they had today.

Beginning in 2018 and ramping up in 2019, another such prognostication combined hype and marketing, and even discussions concerning national trade policies and security that computing experts and the public refrained from warming up to so far: 5G mobile broadband networks. Why care? This one involves how people around the world may (or will) be accessing movies and television shows and ever-larger massive bodies of data over the Internet. At a minimum they will be hearing about 5G until this book goes out of print. 5G is the next generation of telecommunications which promises speeds in mobile broadband of up to 100 times faster than current 4G networks (more hype?). With the wireless market now mature, because everyone who uses Internet services is on 4G, the telecoms need to find new sources of revenue, hence are promoting 5G, and hyping the benefits to customers of the faster network. But, the technology is not sufficiently ready for consumers. They have expressed little interest (so far) in the extra capacity and are happy with their 4G, even in countries with excellent Internet connections.

Yet, as the review of attitudes discussed in this chapter demonstrate, people—largely those most familiar with computing—are able to resist, although not completely avoid, consuming the hubris. They are working their way through the mix of noise and facts, paying attention to continuing developments in the technology, and sorting through how best to use it as tools. Their efforts are complicated by modern society's issues: that new technologies are expensive and so their development often still need to be funded by governments and large and small companies (no longer just individuals), that now hundreds of millions of people are voicing opinions about the role of computing for their children, their politics and their work; that national governments and corporations are using computing to control the views and behaviors of citizens and customers. This is a long list of actions and consequences—the sorts of issues historians, political scientists, sociologists, and economists have studied about earlier technologies. Their experiences demonstrate that humans are just now experiencing the consequences of computing, that they have a long way to go before those have fully manifested themselves, and, as in earlier centuries, effects unpredicted and unknown until they occur.

The hubris and experiences of the past three generations using computers encourages humanity to continue developing this technology and, of course, applying it to all manner of anthropomorphic priorities and actions. So, confidence building hubris is probably less of a problem than one might suppose. If that is the case, what might we suppose might happen next? This is not a question so much about forecasting the emergence of new technologies—technologists pretty much know what will emerge over the next decade since it often takes that long to move fundamental innovations from laboratory to market—than about possibilities for human action and thinking. Speculating is a very human activity, made even more fun and useful in our time because of the availability of so much data, understanding about how to apply scientific principles of investigation, and our technological capability to take an idea and convert it into a tangible object. Hubris suggests that such realities give us choices in which direction computing evolves and its advocates would be right to a certain extent.

However, since so many people are involved in developing and using computing, they also would be wrong. People-machine relations increasingly evolve because of the work of groups and organizations, far less so of individuals such as John von Neumann or a Bill Gates. Bright lights appear in the digital sky like shooting stars for spectacular moments, such as Steve Jobs at Apple and perhaps Mark Zuckerberg at Facebook, but that is what they are—momentary lights in the sky. They only live for one lifetime and only run one or few organizations. There are perhaps bigger forces at work, so we should engage in some exploration of these. That is the purpose of our next chapter.

Chapter 5
How We Might See the End of the Information Age

Let's head straight to the core issue—artificial intelligence, computing that does human-like thinking and action, makes decisions, and ultimately is supposed to be smarter than we mortals. AI as it is called in computer circles has been hyped for over 70 years and for the longest time was the most underperforming, disappointing information technology that never met expectations. Today it seems every book publisher has a book out on AI and every computing journal is discussing it. Yet, it had—and still has—among its defenders some of the smartest human beings, and not all of them crowded together into buildings at their home bases at such universities as the Massachusetts Institute of Technology (MIT), Cal Tech, and Carnegie-Mellon; they were (are) also nested in other universities and inside computer manufacturing firms around the world. AI's high priests occupied a universe wedged somewhere between serious scientific disciplines and science fiction, seemingly weaving back and forth between the two based on how windy the AI hype and discourse was in any particular decade. It seemed in all those years that AI loomed in the background poised almost ready to spring on society. Serious nonfiction books and movies never kept the topic far away from millions of people. But it never pounced, or has it? Hint: Today all manner of firms and government agencies are hiring AI experts; the demand for such skills is borderline insatiable on both sides of the Atlantic, in Russia, and in China and Japan. So, we have to understand what it is, then its implications for people.

The Concept of Artificial Intelligence (AI)

Since most people outside the IT community know little if anything about what today's AI is, we begin with a brief tutorial sufficient for our purposes, but surely not for a serious computer scientist. So be it. For the world at large, it is incumbent on millions of people now to begin learning about this new chapter in the evolution of computing, because finally we may be at the doorstep of a new world that could

© Springer Nature Switzerland AG 2020
J. W. Cortada, *Living with Computers*,
https://doi.org/10.1007/978-3-030-34362-0_5

make all prior developments in computers seem primitive and borderline trivial. It is a remarkable statement to make, especially since every evolution of computing technology has been preceded and then accompanied by great hype, and so we should know better. It turns out we do for certain types of computing, such as our species-wide use of smartphones and increasingly, too, about social media, but far less so about the most sophisticated new developments in information technology. As is often the answer when we ask each other how a relationship is going, with AI "it's complicated."

AI originated in the idea that people could describe human intelligence precisely enough so a computer could be built that could simulate it, hence the idea of *artificial,* as opposed to human intelligence which is normally described as *natural intelligence*, or the real deal. So, already we encounter the notion that intelligence should be described in anthropomorphic terms with human intelligence the benchmark by which to compare all other forms of intelligence.

By that measure, we know, for example, that cockroaches are not as intelligent as humans, even though as a species they have lived far longer than humans believe could happen to their own species. It kicks to the side of the road other intelligence-oriented questions, such as: Is a fern more or less intelligent than a cockroach? Cockroaches have been around for some 320 million years, so clearly able to adapt to massive changes in the world's climate and environment; ferns originated even earlier, some 360 million years ago and in time became a favorite dinosaur meal. Both developed into many types—think anthropomorphically as races—of dramatically different sizes, shapes, and forms.

We humans have only just started to dabble in such diversity over the past 2.5 million years. If the fundamental purpose of intelligence is to make it possible for a species and its individual members to live and procreate, then our anthropomorphic word view needs humbling before the achievements of other living forms and possible future ones, including machines, especially should they someday break away from their human-centric designs. So, conversations about AI really can range all over the place from the serious to the absurd. But there are some core ideas to keep in mind as we size up the effects of computing on our species.

First, there was then and now the dream, the aspiration for AI: that we could augment human intelligence by adding a tool to people's toolbox to assist in their work and play. In the 1950s that aspiration was measured by developing computers that could play chess as well or better than humans. For decades computer scientists worked on this and by the end of the twentieth century they had succeeded to the chagrin of Russian, European, and American chess champions. But by then, AI researchers had also learned that just winning chess or Go was not good enough. The more serious objectives included the fundamental ability of a machine or software that could, like living creatures, understand its environment and optimize or maximize its chances of success, such as staying alive, be healthy, and reproduce itself. To do those things required a system that could consume data (input), learn from it and then formulate plans and actions (outputs) that made it possible for life to continue. Such a worldview prized flexibility and learning.

At the risk of becoming too technical, we should understand one techy term currently bantered about that is increasingly invading conversations about Facebook privacy practices and how online e-business sites target advertisements, or even how government agencies determine if you are a threat to national security: *algorithms.* An algorithm is a set of clearly articulated instructions that dumb computers can execute correctly, software. These can be simple or complex, but can involve multiple sets of instructions interacting with other algorithms. Such rules always applied to games, but in recent decades have been programmed to learn from the data that comes in. For example, if you constantly Google articles about roses, Amazon's computers could be told to start posting advertisements to your computer for things you look up, thus roses and other garden supplies for sale. In medicine current work involves looking at many instances similar to your malady and ruling out possible diagnoses that experience (prior data on cases) suggest are not relevant to the analysis of your condition, and then going further to recommend procedures and treatments that have worked for similar cases before.

The possible applications of algorithms is vast and rapidly becomes complicated, especially as the ability of computers and their sensors to collect data far exceeds human capacity to do so—a situation that already exists. But, scientists have a long way to go in surpassing human intelligence, because algorithms have yet to be developed that can mimic what is known as "commonsense reasoning." People still can think through and process data about time, physical interactions, depth, and space beyond what is possible with computers. We humans expend an enormous amount of our brain work on such subjects, and to that end we allocate about 25% of all our calories fueling our brains.

We need to know more about what AI researchers study. The list is straightforward, however, and includes the following: reasoning and problem solving, how to represent information (knowledge), how to perform planning of all types, learning (what most commentators focus on), processing of human languages so far (perhaps someday being able to communicate with plants), perceptions generated from sensors that collect data about images, temperatures, physical features, smell and so on (useful in speech and vision), motion and manipulation (what robots are about so far), displaying social behaviors such as that displayed by humans (emotion and sentiment), and good old fashion smarts (general intelligence).

In our anthropomorphic world, students of AI engage across multiple academic disciplines—which most scholars and engineers are usually discouraged from doing as there would be too much to know to be effective, so the logic goes—that today is beyond their capacities. They would need to understand computer science, programming, how the human brain works, feedback loops, sociology, and other fields. I contend they would also need to know some history and basic economics to make sense of past successes; philosophers and many theologians would have to weigh in too. We can reasonably use some of our human commonsense intelligence to conclude that the field of AI is very complicated and extremely nebulous. Humans do not like nebulous issues. AI's high priests would love nothing better than to eradicate those conditions and their weapons of choice are algorithms and the collection of inconceivably large bodies of data, the latter gathered today easily and cost-effectively by sensors.

One aspect of AI's current influence is most interesting, known as computational thinking. It is a way of looking at scientific issues that is rapidly taking hold as a style of research and viewing the world. Essentially, it calls for people to build models of whatever natural processes they are studying and then evaluate what those suggest. This approach to doing scientific work represents a departure from long-standing practices of developing theories and conducting experiments. A simple example illustrates the difference. If you wanted to develop a medication to cure a disease, you would first determine what compounds potentially could do the job by feeding these to mice, for instance, and then trying various doses and combinations until you got it right, that is to say, you cured the disease. When thinking computationally, however, you would write a software model that tested through simulation maybe millions of combinations of compounds, getting down to a few that could then be tested on the poor mice. The traditional approach could take years of work, the computational strategy perhaps a few months. The savings in costs and the speed in developing a medicine are huge.

But that is only the first part of thinking computationally. The second involves viewing scientific issues through the lens of information processes. Computer programmers and their compatriots, systems analysts, view their challenge as the act of automating as efficiently as possible an information process, while increasingly scientists and those working in the field of AI flip the issue around and try to write software that attempts to simulate real information processes. They want to replicate by simulation something that happens in the real world, which takes us back to plowing through millions of options to find the right medicine and its dosage for our little mouse, later for we mortals. So, scientists now are asking such questions as: What information process replicates an observed phenomenon, or: What information process is going on in that observed phenomenon? Biologists are keen to understand what is happening between DNA and protein interactions as a step toward creating simulation models of how to alter DNA to cure a disease. Physicists are viewing their world as a collection of information processes, too, also eager to model natural phenomenon. Such an approach makes it possible to test a hypothesis and increase confidence in a theory, even to predict outcomes. All of this takes computer science to a new place in how humans study their own world. In sum, while computer scientists and programmers write algorithms to solve extant problems, scientists are less focused on describing a problem and instead want to observe the behavior of something. The computer experts are using software to do the work of people: play music, show a video, or operate a warehouse for Amazon, while scientists want to continue to do what they have always done: understand how the real world works. For both, AI is yet another tool.

Do not underestimate the worldwide effort underway to use AI. All major fields of human activity are being subjected to AI: healthcare, warfare, driverless cars (aircraft crudely use it today), military weapons, economics, finance, video games, insurance, accounting (largely audits by tax departments), advertising and marketing, scientific research in every sub-discipline, and engineering. The military in advanced economies are committed to AI warfare, including Russia, U.S.A., and China. IBM is betting its future on the power of AI, no longer on just selling computers made out of metal and silicon-based computer chips. Progress is being made all over the place with AI. It is nearly impossible to find a major development in the world of DNA today—and they are coming fast and furious—without seeing the use of AI. Improvements in the treatment of cancer being made right now owe much to the use of AI methods.

Understanding the difference between AI and what computers have long been able to do, what makes them "dumb" at the same time in the minds of computer scientists, requires us to appreciate the difference. A hypothetical almost ridiculous example might help. If we could attach a "fix the flat tire machine" to our car, we could instruct it through normal computing to fix a flat when it occurs, teaching it how to do that. Sensors on all four wheels would feed continuous data to the machine's computer about, say, air pressure and when it notes that air pressure is declining, even though it might not know in which tire. So, the computer would reach into its instructions prepared by humans who had anticipated the problem and find that since it was not told which tire to replace (that can't be anticipated in advance), it would change all four of them, confident that through that process the flat tire would have been replaced.

In a more AI-centered "fix the flat tire machine," its computer would have been taught how to identify which tire was losing air, and by exchanging information with kindred machines attached to millions of automobiles, would learn over time which of our tires tended to lose air and when it would make sense to replace one, perhaps even before it went completely flat. It would inform all the other tire fixing machines in the country as to which tire it changed, why, and how. That information would then inform the other machines to anticipate similar behavior and then to take action. Of course, there is no value judgment yet taking place here the way a human would might factor into all these decisions and actions, such as accounting for the changing conditions of the road as they were being encountered, knowledge about the age of the tires, the ability of the driver, age of the vehicle, and so forth. AI people would say all of those other factors represent the next evolution in AI.

We won't get into a discussion here about what critics have to say about the future of AI, such as potential loss of jobs, devaluation of humans, and so forth, because much of that has yet to unfold. We will come back to some of those issues, however, in the last chapter. For the moment, it is enough to understand what AI is at an elementary level and that it is evolving rapidly from failed and disappointing uses to effective ones that already affect our daily activities. In the process it is redefining the nature of computing, even making the word computing increasingly outdated, all of which leads to the fundamental idea posed by the title of this chapter. But, we have other issues to travel through first.

The Case That We Live in the Information Age

The best names for an age in history are invented after most everyone in that age has died: Age of the French Revolution, Victorian Age, Gilded Age, New Deal. The labels that don't work out well are ones people create during their lifetimes: Atomic Age, Cold War era. The problem, of course, is that once you tag a period, everyone and everything gets an image that emphasizes a feature that may not be accurate, is simply found not to be true, or trivial. For those readers old enough to have lived in the 1950s (Nuclear Age) did you spend a lot of time with nuclear energy or even worrying about nuclear war? Did you use nuclear energy to make most of your electricity? What about those of you who lived in the 1970s and 1980s, during the Cold War? Admittedly that rivalry between the Soviets and the Americans was more serious, but really, did that label define your actions, your identity? You were too busy being in elementary or high school, doing your job at work, buying groceries and diapers, taking care of children, pets, and grandparents. To be candid, you would be hard pressed to find an historian who wants to label any period unless, of course, they are trying to sell a book they wrote (e.g., the Age of Jackson) or a commentator of modern events, such as Shoshana Zuboff, *The Age of Surveillance Capitalism*, that her publisher brought out in 2019. When someone does this, it is to highlight a thesis, a point of view, or to appease the marketing department at their publisher's office.

Arguments in favor of giving a period an Age name are few and superficially compelling. A name gives a period or group an identity that is a short hand summary of the period: Jazz Age for the 1920s when the American economy was booming, women got the right to vote and were more liberated to smoke cigarettes, drink, and go on un-chaperoned dates. Even novel twists in language helped, such as labeling 17 million American veterans of World War II as the Greatest Generation. Labels stimulated behavior, such as extending further reverence to World War II veterans, all of them. It stimulates an emphasis on a particular point of view. The Age of Jackson has been popular with historians because in Andrew Jackson's time as president (1820s–1830s), American national politics evolved fundamentally toward what we practice today: two party national elections, campaigning, even fake news and insults hurled at each other, a sharp break from prior experience when these behaviors were nonexistent or minor. The British Victorian Age conveniently swept up whole collections of images: specific styles of furniture and the way men and women dressed, how Western society was organized, favorite books, life styles, and political views. Western Civilization has been handy for over a century for suggesting a common look-and-feel for a cluster of countries: Christianity, physically located largely in Europe for twenty centuries, shared Roman experience (but really only true around the Mediterranean), Protestant Revolution, and so forth.

If a middle class Japanese, North American, or West European were able to go back in time, say to the 1920s—one century ago—and walk through the house or apartment of an ancestor, they would have noticed some differences. The apartment or house would have probably been smaller than the one they occupy today; in the USA easily a third smaller. In the American one there would have been a small bookcase, probably 3–4 shelves, each one about 2 feet long filled with a Bible, probably also a dictionary, a few catalogs, several novels, and miscellaneous other books dealing with medicine, gardening, or farming. That household would have subscribed to the local weekly newspaper, perhaps even a magazine or two. By the end of the 1930s almost every household would have had an AM radio. In the United States and in a tiny number of European cities, a nearby public library would have given people access to a few thousand books, dozens of magazines, and a handful of newspapers. All of one's personal files would have fit into one or few cardboard boxes or even a drawer or two. People would have talked to neighbors and experts to gather information before making decisions. It was all a fairly low key affair with little organized amounts of information available to a resident.

Fast forward to 1990—just before the availability of the Internet to the masses—and you would notice a few more changes. The dwellings in North America would have increased in square footage, those in other countries not as much, but still some. There would have been more books in the house and apartment, the same number of newspapers but probably a few more subscriptions to magazines. Home owners would have had access to more radio stations by now and probably through more than one radio at home, another in each of their automobiles. They also had television, which provided news on a regular schedule, information programs (such as about cooking, history, and gardening), and more sports than the radio. More dramatic than radio, TV offered images, hence the ability to broadcast events as they unfolded, soap operas and comedy programs serving up misleading if idealized reflections of society. Americans would recall the experience of watching television the entire weekend following the assassination of John F. Kennedy in November 1963, the landing of men on the Moon in 1969 as they did it, and shocking war footage in color of the Vietnam War in the 1970s. Both at home and at work they would have relied on increased amounts of organized information with which to do an increasing amount of school study and office work, and more to make decisions than in the 1920s and 1930s. The years of formal education on all three continents would have increased by several years; it seemed most people now had at least gone to high school.

Travel further in time to today and what would you see? The big changes would have been the arrival of the Internet on a global basis, what we have discussed earlier in this book; access to this now vast collection of information in one's hand or strapped to your ear by blue tooth technology; a clutter of digital devices at home and work: PCs, laptops, tablets, old mobile phones with dead batteries in a desk drawer, at least one smartphone that worked, handheld calculators, streaming Internet content into several TV sets, portable music devices with headsets to which one could stream music, e-books, or podcasts while jogging or riding a bus. In short, for most of our waking hours we wallow in a world of input and feedback, of communications and information.

Is it any wonder then that when a commentator on television, a book writer, or a friend declares that we live in an Information Age, we are inclined to agree? He or she is, in fact, correct. We do rely on greater amounts of information with which to go through life's activities; researchers are expected to study more data than ever; we have more information ephemera than ever, and, of course, various generations and types simultaneously, books and smartphones, tablets and magazines. The argument is straightforward and seemingly obvious: more of us work in offices handling information than we do on farm fields, digging ditches, when we are outdoors, or on factory floors. We require more formal education and the ability to use digitally-enhanced equipment than ever before. It is not good enough that a factory worker can drill a hole into a piece of metal with a handheld drill; that person has to be able to operate a numerical controlled device from a PC screen that is a complex drill press to do the work on ever larger numbers of metal parts.

This all happened so fast that most people over the age of 45 can remember a time when they had less information and relied equally less on it to go about their lives. That's over 2 billion people (as of 2018). That year worldwide, 58% of humanity was between the ages of 15 and 54. Those under the age of 35 have lived without ever knowing a time without the Internet. The percentages are higher for residents in all Northern Hemisphere countries. Because cities were always hotbeds of information activity, and urban dwellers experienced that, it helps to know that about 55% of all humanity lives in towns. The fastest growing cities in the world are located in India, China, Africa and parts of Latin America, so over 3 billion urbanites are being exposed faster to the availability of information than their parents or grandparents. One does not need a distinguished professor from Oxford, Harvard, or the University of Tokyo to tell them that they live in an Information Age. They experience it, they are convinced that they "get it."

The Case That We Do Not Live in the Information Age

Just as there are arguments for naming an age, there are others arraigned against that perspective. Most historians avoid naming an age, and I am with them. The most fundamental problem with naming a period is that the name exaggerates one feature of the time at the expense of others. For example, the Victorian Age was not dominated by Queen Victoria, except perhaps in England, but certainly not in other European countries where even the average citizen may not have known who she was, such as peasants in Russia or the poor in Spain and Italy, all of whom were experiencing life styles that had not changed from pre-Victorian times. Misleading can conjure up false images of what actually happened. If you are going to name an age, it should at least be after some activity which is widely practiced or with which the majority of people identify. By the first criteria then life in the United States since the 1930s should be labeled the Age of the Potato or Corn because of the widespread continuous consumption of spuds and corn. But, of course, that would be ridiculous; it would leave out too many other defining events, such as World War II or Vietnam. The Space Age petered out when the Americans stopped going to the Moon, leaving that age to have survived as a name for barely two decades. Historians rightfully argue that there were many events and behaviors that coursed simultaneously through a society in any period, so selecting one feature just gets in the way of understanding the full scope of what happened.

Then there is the ever popular Western Civilization, which led even properly trained historians to examine most human activities through Eurocentric perspectives the way our species took an anthropomorphic view of all realities. The great belief (actually myth) is that the West got rich because Europeans were smarter and invented capitalism and, of course had guns; Asia was backward, Indians in South

America were uncivilized and fought with bows and arrows; Western armies were more "advanced" than anyone else's, and so forth. It took over a century for historians to begin realizing that all these perspectives were factually wrong. They are still crawling out of that misleading paradigm just as China is resuming its historic primacy in human history.

So let's briefly make the argument for why we do not live in an Information Age. Historians would argue that every era was underpinned by information, normally thinking of organized, written-down facts that had to be consulted on papyrus, paper, and now screens. They noted rising rates of literacy in Asia, Europe and Latin America over the past 500 years to demonstrate the growing number of people who could read and write, who learned by that process to collect and to expect information of use to them to be organized in accessible ways. They point out that information became less expensive over time, even in eighteenth century France and Germany, certainly so by the mid-nineteenth century in the United States. By 1500 over a million printed books had flooded across Europe; in each year of the nineteenth century more books were published than the year before in the United States. Similar trends were documented for most of Northern Europe. Even in the Dark Ages of the Middle Ages, when most literate people were essentially a handful of priests and lawyers, far more individuals were literate and used texts in China and Japan. Once they started looking at the issue of literacy, history of books, writing and information, historians discovered it all over the place. Now entire history journals are devoted to the history of information; few of the articles they contain focus on the Internet and screens—yet.

A second argument links back to our discussion about naming Ages. We still eat a great number of potatoes. Until the early 1500s only Indians largely in Peru ate potatoes. Then Spanish conquistadores introduced spuds to Europe. But it took the horrible years of the Thirty Years War (1618–1648) in Central Europe to convince people that invading armies would not dig up their supplies of potatoes as readily as they would confiscate their wheat and farm animals. In the seventeenth and eighteenth centuries Europeans discovered that the nutritional content of potatoes was high, while the Irish demonstrated a person could live off a combination of spuds and dairy products. So, for over 300 years many people ate potatoes, but we do not refer to European history from, say, 1640 to the present as the Age of Spuds, because there were too many other things going on that lent their names to an age. These included wars, reigns of monarchs, and political movements. It turns out that in our Age of Information, we too had more going on than eating French fries or staring at our screens. Recently, historians may have actually stumbled on a comprehensive umbrella tag for a period: The Little Ice Age (1600s–1700s), when in fact for over a century, the world got colder with profound effects on *all* aspects of life. But it took them over 250 years and a great deal of scientific discoveries about climate change to arrive at that label.

For your consideration during the period in which computers existed, we had World War II, Korean War, numerous civil wars in Africa after 1960, the Vietnam War, Cold War, Bosnia, and genocide in Asia and Africa. The world lost over 80 million people due to wars, just in the twentieth century. In the same period we had the

Green Revolution, by which billions of people could be fed rice, corn and wheat in Asia, Africa and America, thanks to genetically modified seeds. We had our assortment of political leaders that could lend themselves to ages named after them, such as Stalin, Roosevelt, Churchill, and Queen Elizabeth II, among others. These events and rulers were consistent with what in earlier times were appropriate *noms d'une époque*. But, humans had too much going on to settle on one feature of their time as emblematic of all that they did. To do so would, again, have been misleading.

A third argument that is just appearing goes something like this. As computing became smaller and more versatile, sophisticated and nuanced, it is being embedded in all manner of activities and objects—a point we have made earlier. Increasingly, computing is becoming anonymous, invisible, out of sight embedded in other devices and objects, buried underground, hidden behind walls like electrical wires, or invisible as data is wirelessly transmitted, say, from your home PC to your printer at the other end of the house—still pure magic to me, but that electrical engineers and computer scientists can rationally explain. You don't see it, so you think less about its effects on your life, just as you don't think that much about the oxygen you breathe several times during every minute of your life. Like breathing or the furniture in your home, it is just there. When something becomes like plumbing and we pay hardly any attention to it, we becomes less conscious of its existence. When that happens, we are less influenced by these through our conscious behavior. It has moved to our subconscious and so no longer considered a candidate to name an age after, as in the human brain where certain functions are allocated to a pretty automatic process—such as breathing and regulating heart rates in the brainstem.

My half century of observing how people dealt with information and computing leads me to conclude that we no more live in an Age of Information than did spud eating Europeans in the eighteenth and nineteenth centuries, but all were increasingly being influenced by the rapid discovery of scientific, engineering, medical, and economic facts. That does not mean the earlier period and our own are the same—far from it. Historians may well look back on the late twentieth and all of the twenty-first centuries as a sped-up extension of human reliance on information and the tools with which these were delivered, extending a trend that began at least with the arrival of the Enlightenment and even earlier at the dawn of scientific practices.

Why the Issue Is Important

If I am correct, there are a number of consequences and issues to think about—the subject of our last chapter—some of which make sense to introduce now. Carried to its logical conclusion, it is the fact that we are using more computing, more sensors, and thinking increasingly about such topics as privacy and the uses of social media that is making information ubiquitous, almost as we think of the air we breathe. In other words, the more information with which we envelop ourselves, the less distinguishing the notion of an Information Age becomes. It is thus ubiquitous, ordinary, not distinguished by some uniqueness. We move on to the next area of evolution, perhaps to addressing climate change or getting serious about colonizing other planets and moons, issues that engage the cerebrum parts of our brains. We periodically pause, of course, to focus on such issues as cleaning up the air, installing some new form of computing and cogitating about its implications (e.g., biologically-based computing instead of our old metal, plastic and silicon ones), and fighting wars over ideology, religion, and economics. But as the world becomes more wired up, more functioning as a sensor-driven environment managed by AI, it will seem that life on earth is less about computing. That may seem counter intuitive, but we think about our times and how we will live them largely by what we focus on in a *conscious* way. If you are at war you think and act about that war; if you are in love, thoughts about living in an Information Age disappear as you focus on a single individual.

We already know what is driving us toward an era where we discuss information less and focus more on other matters. AI and computerized sensors are the most immediate and obvious influencers; so too portable electricity (energy) that can be placed where needed, either with batteries or technologies that generate it by various means.

Does this mean we lose (give up) our jobs or that society—Earth—will make it possible to spend all our time at the beach swimming and playing with friends and relatives? For decades too many futurists predicted that our work weeks would shorten, that we would all be paid a salary by the government for just existing, and that for many work was no longer necessary. Some were marginally correct: work weeks shortened over the past 150 years, Finland experimented giving people a base salary, but we all still work, children still need to be educated, too many people cannot abide just sitting around doing little or nothing, and individuals are curious enough to want to find solutions to new problems. All of that is going on before we even consider that our societies and religions call upon us not to just hang out at the beach all day. The value systems humans developed to survive and thrive over many hundreds of thousands of years will not be overturned so quickly to be replaced by one in which humans are cuddled by computers, sensors, and their robotic henchmen. It turns out, people are very anthropomorphic.

Which brings us back to the human activity of being tool users. That turns the circle back to the question of how AI plays in the evolution of modern society. I contend that AI, like climate change, attraction to a child or to a new loved one, is something humans should pay attention to, at least during the lifetimes of today's adults. Perhaps after they have passed on, AI will pay attention to its AI forms, possibly initially in some old fashion anthropomorphic form before evolving into a yet not understood one. But that leads us to science fiction when we are here focused on today's realities. Experts observing the current transition occurring with computers are pretty much in agreement that over the next couple of decades we will be doing a great deal with AI, robotics, and drones. The latter is just now getting off the ground, robotics is morphing from industrial to consumer forms, and AI is transforming all manner of objects into more intelligent cognitive tools for we humans, and more able to learn and then to take actions based on new findings. We will still see all of these forms of computing as tools for our use. Looking at the technology through our self-centered anthropomorphic lens, the most pervasive of all is AI. Because AI is going to be an ever so important influence in human affairs, we are going to have to wade in the weeds a bit to understand what is already emerging, so apologies in advance, if necessary.

Emerging Types of AI Tools

There are essentially a half dozen collections of tools (mostly software) considered part of the AI universe. It is enough to briefly identify them to give us a sense of their impending role, indeed value to organizations and later to individuals. They are in various stages of development and use and, if I am allowed an opinion, still primitive. But that is all changing, too, as we apply both human and AI experience to the task of creating even more advanced uses of AI. With such developments, we can expect that the words *computing* and *computers* will drop from our vocabulary, relics of the late twentieth and early twenty-first centuries. It would not be the first time that happened. Who uses ague instead of malaria, horseless carriage instead of car, apothecary instead of pharmacist, or condition instead of social position? All were in use during the early twentieth century.

It also happens with information technology words, phrases no longer used but that anyone over the age of 55 encountered: electronic brains before we settled on computer, floppy disks, DOS, tape drives, and Cobol, just as we no longer say icebox rather refrigerator, yet we still store data in portable devices, use operating systems, even magnetic tape some times, and after Y2K in 2000, many software programs written in Cobol that people have yet to get around to converting to some other "computer language." And who even says World Wide Web anymore? So, how AI is described today will probably seem quaint in a decade or two because the number and speed of transformations in AI technology are greater than in the past. But the notion that AI is a tool box probably will not.

One class of tools already in use are searches and optimizations. Software can be used to logically reason through piles of data to find answers and specific pieces of information. The wicked speed of a computer—which can search for data faster and more thoroughly than the human mind—also lends itself to optimizing tasks we ask of the technology. When combined with mathematical thinking AI offers a second tool: applied logic. This is the idea that computing can help solve problems, mathematical or otherwise, as in business to optimize the selection of a new store front or most efficient (or fastest) way to deliver goods. When used this way AI builds on over 2000 years of thinking about logic, although it has a ways to go, especially if it confronts preexisting rules in a computer about how to deal with a situation. Applying what we now know about probability theories are already useful additions to the AI toolbox. These help in reasoning, learning, perceptions, and planning. Combined with mathematics, this is already a well-used tool in making decisions (i.e., called decision trees) in science, engineering, government policy planning, and in business.

Probability is pretty interesting when matched up with tons of data. For example, have you ever wondered how Google could provide translations for a phrase in so many languages? Here is the secret. First Google has collected millions upon millions of words and phrases in many languages—call it Big Data. Second, it takes the phrase or sentence that you want translated and compares it to definitions, words and expressions in the language you want to translate to and calculates the probability that a phrase in one language has a high percentage chance of matching your phrase. It cannot speak Spanish, Japanese, or any other language, it just calculates probabilities. If the probability of a match is high enough (determined by the programmer of the translating tool as to what is "high enough") it gives that to you. It can do that because computers work so fast now that it seems to you to be an almost instantaneous translation when in fact it is a math problem being solved.

Have you noticed how these translations have gotten better, too, over the years? That is because it takes the work it did for you and adds it to its collection of earlier translations and ever-growing body of foreign language texts so that when the next person asks for a similar translation, it can give him or her a greater odds on chance of getting right the translated text, or at least more right than before. Magic? Not really, its probability, mathematics, lots of data, and high speed computing, but it is wondrous, nonetheless.

We now turn to the whole topic of networks. Two ideas are emerging as entire collections of new AI tools. Drawing on thinking about how the brain works, neural networks comprise collections of data (ideas) sent from one part of the brain to another. Trying to do that with computers dates to even before the dawn of computers. It is in this general topical area that notions of feedback either in one direction or back and forth, for example, are entwined in computing, often using the language of mathematics to facilitate the digital conversation. The role of neural networks is still emerging, while these have been the subject of much investigation when applied in AI. The second related topic is the notion we have already talked about: that the entire world is rapidly becoming one huge integrated neural system—or brain— thanks to the deployment of the Internet to collect, analyze, and communicate information in such vast quantities that the individual human brain cannot contain. While that last sentence sounds like science fiction, it is incrementally becoming a reality that gives promise to more successful applications of neural networks in the coming years. When we talk about such networks, we are going beyond just anthropomorphic concepts of thinking, to what increasingly scientists see happens with all living matter. That can be a step in the direction that an early pioneer of computing, Alan Turing, suggested in the 1930s, when he argued that we should focus less on whether a computer can think and instead, "decide if a machine can act as intelligently as a human being." Ultimately, AI tools need to do work relevant to humans.

There are two other activities often mixed in with AI to keep in mind, because they represent practical uses of AI already being implemented. The first is an old idea—pattern recognition. Humans are superb in recognizing patterns, better than computers, so far. We use all manner of terms to describe what humans do: apply tacit knowledge, are wise, use their experience, and "connect the dots." Older people are often deemed wiser than younger folks, even though the latter may have better memories, think and talk faster. Computers are increasingly learning to recognize patterns, such as about traffic on streets or in the movement of the planets, your Google searches that lead to suggested advertising aimed at you and your interests, and so forth. Pattern recognition software rely on many of the AI tools cataloged above. The second activity is the massive collection of information discussed before that, then, a computer can scrub through to identify patterns. That is simply the act of applying lots of electronic computer muscle power to plow through the data.

A reality check for us: today electronic sensors collect and pass through the Internet vastly more information than do all humans on earth. In the second decade of the twenty-first century people became a minority on the Internet, even as more of them gained access to this network. One would be hard pressed to find an IT expert who thinks sensors will only collect the same amount of data as they do today; their expectation is that there will be orders of magnitude more for sensors to gather, study, and apply. The day will soon come when we simply will not know how many sensors there are and we will not care. These two functions are already being done today. With that base of information coming in, combined with the need for pattern recognition, the other AI tools already identified can then be applied, and that is before any others we are yet to invent in the next couple of decades.

So far humans are in charge of how computers (AI) work; they still set the agendas—the work plans—for these technologies. We can comfortably think that this will remain the case for some time because the promise of AI has both a bad track record of not delivering on the hype, which will encourage people who do the actual work of implementing AI to be cautious and thorough, and we know enough about the nuts-and-bolts of computing to recognize there is so much more research and development yet to come along. All of this is happening as every aspect of computing's technology—theory, components, machines, software—are still transforming at rates comparable to what happened over the past seven decades.

Everything in computing affects everything else, so as changes in one aspect of computing occurs, it often affects other features that were unanticipated. For example, until computerized data storage dropped massively in cost and could be increased in volume, beginning in the 1960s, one could only imagine uses of pattern recognition applications. Now it is real, but with the advancement of all manner of digital (intelligent) sensors, the quantity of data collected is forcing users to catch up with the mathematics and other thinking about how best to harvest insights from this jumble of electronic impulses. This is why almost every issue of the Computer Society's magazine, *Computer*, or *Wired* read like status reports on technological transformations and almost as sci-fi literature. But these are great perches from which to see what is happening, often presented in the kind of English those of us who only have a flirting relationship with computer technologies can understand. The humans still rule.

So, Does This Mean We Might See the End of the Information Age?

With all this additional computing pouring in on us how we view our world and the role of information helps shape our agenda of activities at the individual, job, company, industry, and global levels. Our perspectives always have, so we are back to the debate the French had in the 1960s and 1970s about how they saw their society evolve and what they wanted to see happen. If almost every device is computerized, if even clothes and furniture are embedded with "intelligence" (already happening), if sensors are everywhere (many pets have chips in them, so too patients suffering from dementia) the word computer becomes meaningless. If we stop using that word, even of thinking about computing as we go about our daily lives, what effect does that decline in the use of those terms have on our perceptions about Information Ages? For the past half century we linked concepts of Information Age to that of computers and telecommunications; the Europeans did it the most with notions of ICT (information and communications technologies) and telematics. So, as computers as independent stand-alone devices morph even more intensely into our popup toasters and coffee makers, into our cars and clothing, will we see notions of Information Ages also vanish? While impossible to predict for sure, just the fact that we raise the question already points to changes.

The most obvious is the same when we do not consider ourselves as living in the Age of the Potato or the Age of Breathing Oxygen. When something becomes as ubiquitous as potato consumption and breathing, humans look for new identities and activities. This behavior proffers opportunities both wonderful and uncertain, of course, but at a minimum serves up changes. Do we focus on climate change control, colonization of new planets and stars, finally resolve the 500+ year guerrilla war between Christian religious beliefs and scientific practices, or do we use AI to launch the Mother of All Wars and simply blow ourselves up? Computational R&D will continue, because humans are voracious consumers of all manner of data and favor, using technologies in support of that central human activity. Life for all living creatures is possible because of data "inputs" and "outputs."

Discussions about Information Ages in the 1960s–1980s evolved around improving the quality of life, safety, and the health of humankind. The evidence overwhelmingly supports the conclusion that humans improved their lives in the past century, as measured by worldwide declining rates of crime, survival from diseases, increased longevity of life, improved levels of quality of life, and pursuit of happiness. All of these developments emerged from our species having access to more knowledge and information, and to its better application of those to the human condition. Computing contributed to that process in dramatic fashion before whatever is coming next with AI and new forms of information processing. To do otherwise would counter the selfishness of humanity's desire to do what is best for itself. So, perhaps we should contemplate life in a post-Age of Information World. We take up that challenge in the next chapter.

Chapter 6
Life in a Post-information Age Era?

What are we to make of the human-computer relationship of the past eight decades? What about the next half century? Technologies of all kinds have sway over our thinking, imposing on we humans an intellectual hegemony, and not just simply the weaker paradigm of thinking scientifically. Technological progress is a near God-like belief in large swaths of the world, even after accounting for such nastiness as computer chip toxins infiltrating our aquifers, nuclear plants exposing nearby communities to radiation in Russia and Japan, smart bombs killing civilians in regional wars, or fake news disseminated by bots. Computers made possible massive increases in economic prosperity, superior and safer travel in all forms, rapid and sophisticated development of medicines and new scientific information, enriched the lives of children with fun "screen time," their parents too if we are to be candid, and made enormous amounts of information available to all of us "just in time." Our Experience Economy would simply not function without information technologies, or our impatience to enjoy it.

But there are limits to the power of technology. For example, Europe and the United States had the world's most technologically advanced collection of weapons in human history during the Twentieth century. Yet after 1945, Europe lost all its colonies in a half generation after spending a half millennium acquiring them. The United States could not achieve a definitive victory in the Korean War in the 1950s, despite its stunning defeat of Japan and Nazi Germany in collaboration with allies a decade earlier. The United States failed again in Vietnam during the 1960s–1970s against what was arguably a militarily backward enemy. Military historians draw the lesson that technology is never—was never—enough. Nations had to have sound strategies applied effectively using one's strengths and that mitigated weaknesses. Optimized leadership and logistics, collaboration, and warfare also were important. Winning nations had economic and social assets that allowed them to "stick it out" long enough to wear out the other side; that is how the U.S. "won" the Cold War against the Soviet Union. In other words, anthropomorphically-oriented technologies without the capabilities of humans were never enough. A rifle in the hands of a poorly trained sixteenth century European soldier was not as effective against a

© Springer Nature Switzerland AG 2020   59
J. W. Cortada, *Living with Computers*,
https://doi.org/10.1007/978-3-030-34362-0_6

skilled Chinese warrior with a bow and arrow who had deep knowledge of the local terrain. The cases exist in every age all over the world.

Existential forces must be accounted for and the European empire builders teach us that lesson. Spanish conquistadors in South America did not conquer the area because of outstanding military technologies, or even good tactics. They won because over 80% of the Indians they encountered caught smallpox and other European diseases from them or worked under brutal slave conditions and so died off within roughly one century. Those two realities left the continent wide open to those Spaniards who had immunity from these germs and in need of African slaves to fill labor voids. In Africa, it was the reverse, where modern weapons were no match for local diseases that killed so many Portuguese that the best they could do was huddle along the beaches and trade goods for slaves with local tribes immune to indigenous germs. So, beware the hubris of IT exceptionalism. It's good stuff to read, but not perfect, and in all probability, dangerously misleading.

Second, because we have so much information and its gadgetry, we might forget a central observation of this book: that all this new IT is an add-on to the core activities of humankind, even though it is highly integrated into all manner of our species' pursuits. Humans have used information for over a million years, yet, we also need to keep in mind that we have enhanced their activities in the past 5000 years with data handling tools. Computers began to change that balance of power between who controlled the tools, starting a slow shift from people dictating how they were to be used to the tools themselves beginning to shape what people did with them—the AI story just beginning to unfold today. So, we live in a messy, ambiguous time when we find it difficult to see what the road ahead looks like for humankind.

The purpose of this chapter is to suggest considerations to keep in mind as we think about our immediate future relationship with computing over the next several decades. At the risk of making this serious discussion too simple, I would like to proceed with several interconnected discussions. I want to begin by exploring what gives AI authority over humans, then describe its known limitations and shaping powers. I argue for why focusing on the role of information is more useful than concentrating on its underlying technology. That discussion neatly takes us to non-computer issues of a humanistic nature from cyborgs to the singularity, to biological forms, and ends with an assessment of how all these developments fit into the realm of religion. There is a great deal of material to cover, but they are tightly related to each other so we have little choice on how best to proceed.

What Makes Emerging AI a Controlling Force

Even though previous chapters demonstrated that we mortals deal with all manner of computing, the central conversation today is all about AI, and how it is changing the nature of our dependence on computing in ways imaginable only by computer scientists and sci-fi writers a half century ago. Stephen Wolfram, one of the world's most highly respected experts on computational thinking, made the point that all the questions which the computer could not answer in the movie *Desk Set* in 1957 were answered by his research team using computers by 2009. Two lessons are obvious: AI is progressing to a critical point of effectiveness and that significant progress takes far longer than most pundits understand. Keep those two points in mind when later we discuss the possibilities of machines becoming smarter than us, of we becoming cyborgs, and of computers replacing the human race on earth (or possibly just in Space).

When we are forced to fill out all fields in a form online before we can gain access to information, a service or product, we are being controlled by AI. When we see only advertisements at our frequently visited websites related to our recent web searches, we are being manipulated by AI. When we see fake news or biased reporting about an issue, others are using AI to influence our thinking. When someone believes a bad political trend is unfolding and is incited to protest, riot, or even shoot someone, that person is being cajoled by AI. All that happens today worldwide even though computer scientists strive for noble reasons to understand intelligent behavior then design it into computing. We have reached the point where some AI-driven computing is rationale, that is to say, it can learn to improve its behavior to meet objectives set for it by humans, such as what increasingly is happening with robotics in manufacturing. The objectives can be noble, such as promoting positive behavior, effective learning by people, etc.; or it can serve darker purposes, as in controlling political behavior and promoting views by a dictatorship.

Effectiveness can be faulty too. An example often cited by AI scientists is if you tell a brilliantly effective machine to optimize the manufacture of paperclips without carefully building into the software instructions with limiting guardrails, the system in theory would marshal all the metal in the world to do just that, resulting in humanity losing all other metal objects: cars, forks and knives, and our hammers of course. That would happen because computers have yet to develop judgment, like humans have who would, upon seeing a computer start to turn the world into a pile of paperclips would make a midcourse correction to limit how many of these were manufactured. We could see the same happen with, say, trying to cure a human disease, with AI electing to use all people as experimental guinea pigs, or to clean up the oceans, consuming all the oxygen on our planet to do the job, leaving humanity breathless and extinct. Oops.

As AI's role increases in our everyday lives, the ability of computing to make decisions increases. Until humanity learns to teach AI-based systems how to make better decisions, we will experience controlling AI increasing. We see this today when we call an automated system at a bank, pharmacy, or help desk, when we have to choose all kinds of options on an automated phone call, or when a system forces us to make certain decisions, instead of what we want to do is scream into the phone "I want to speak to a live customer service person." How we align the behavior of an AI-driven machine to our human needs and values remains a challenge and until resolved, technology's controlling features can only exist and be used. It is the limitations of AI that fosters its more controlling features. Of course, even if those limitations were overcome, a dictator or a dishonest person could still program AI to implement their nefarious human values. So, as with so many prior human technologies, AI can be a controlling force for good and evil.

Limits and Problems of AI as Shaping Forces

We have already identified one limit (or problem) with AI—the risk that it could go off and do things out of scope with human intentions: too many paper clips, consumes Earth's oxygen, allows a dictator to manage our thoughts and actions. The risk that AI spins out of control is increased by the fact that its evolution is happening very fast. While it took humans and other living creatures millions of years to evolve, so as to thrive in their existing ecosystems, AI has gone from concept to reality in less than a century with no end in sight. The "AI Risk" as it is known is the specter that we might improve AI too fast without the guard railing that evolution's slow moving pace was able to build into living creatures.

So, what we might be creating with our information technologies is artificial stupidity, a low IQ form of AI. Bots cranking out dumb or wrong messages during the U.S. elections in 2016 and European ones in 2018, without the software having any understanding of what it was doing really is, well, stupid. If those messages are accepted as truth by people ill-equipped to differentiate reality from fabrication, then we have another form of stupidity (or ignorance): human stupidity. Adjusting for that possibility increasingly is catching the attention of computer scientists as an important research priority.

If you are thinking that perhaps AI yet is not as smart as you are, the situation is even worse. Psychologists are beginning to realize that even 4-year old children can think through some issues better than current AI systems. AI can gather a great deal of information, analyze it to identify statistically what are its patterns and report those out. That requires a lot of computing and electricity to help a human define and solve a problem. The child has a far more diverse body of knowledge about their world than a computer, hence, context, making decisions on fewer, but more diverse sets of data (input) than an AI system. Computers need lots of data, a 4-year old only a few examples to generalize about a situation to take action. Over time, more examples—but less than an AI system needs—enriches the context in which a child makes decisions. A child can infer from whatever they know, computers cannot yet do that. Children make assumptions about their world and issues, computers do not yet do that either. Even more intriguing, we do not know how humans do it. Children are social and so learn by imitating older kids and observing adults and practicing, absorbing and thinking about what is happening, not just simply obeying parents or other adults. It is why your child will rebel against limits set on their screen time, while a computer will say, "OK, you do not want me to spend more time on a video game, fine, I will obey" without having given any thought about the implications of its decision.

Our discussion leads to a crucial point: that because humans are discriminating thoughtful creatures, they cannot yet rely on computing beyond a point where they personally conclude there are objectives and practices they will or cannot tolerate. Since there are no creditable forecasts as to when computers will be able to match a 4 year old child's ability to discern and discriminate in a thoughtful manner that takes into account all kinds of messy types of data, AI has its limitations. Even the ability to craft useful hypotheses upon which to gather data and to make thoughtful decisions is beyond the current ability of AI.

If you ask a child of 6 or 8 years of age how to build a tower 8 feet high out of a pile of wooden building blocks, as I have done with my grandsons, they create hypotheses about how to proceed that has nothing to do with such logical pieces of data as the number and dimensions of the blocks. In our case, they made such assumptions as, "let's not build the tower on the carpet, because the rug is not steady-enough to support it after a certain height," or, "let's build it in the corner of the room, where nobody can accidently bump into it when they bring groceries through to the kitchen." Their hypotheses were: rugs are an unstable foundation, people shake the floor or come too close to a tower as they walk from the garage to the kitchen. Nobody taught them to consider those conditions; but we would have to do that to an AI system if we wanted it to be as good as these children. Or, and this is the hard part, teach the AI system whatever skills these children have that scientists have yet to understand sufficiently to implant into a computer.

Putting Information Back into Its Historic Place

We are so anthropomorphic, really. From the earliest times when people thought about machines to do thinking work, they quickly navigated to analogies with the human brain. The first books about computing published in the early 1950s spoke about "Giant Brains;" even our brilliant mathematician Professor Wiener thought in terms of biological feedback mechanisms interacting with brains. We have never left that analogy behind. Throughout this book and any that you read by psychologists and computer scientists about AI and about other features of computing always have human brains in mind. Almost all benchmarks of "good," "bad," "effective," or "advanced" computers or AI are made in comparison to the capabilities of the human brain. And why not? We are more interested in the wellbeing of our species than of any machine. For thousands of years as a species we augmented our capabilities with external tools: eyeglasses to see better, shoes to protect our feet, canes so we could walk in old age, dental implants, knee replacements, nose jobs to improve breathing, hair implants, the list is endless. Computers, like handheld adding machines, support our brains that are hidden behind our re-crafted noses and blanketed by our shock of implanted hair follicles. It was always about us. Since it was always about us, then let's talk about us again.

We overtly and subconsciously need information with which to go about living life safely, successfully, and long. As a species we came to realize that when humans gained the ability to write and read, to keep records, publish books, send kids to school, to move from superstition to religious beliefs and now to the practice of science—all intellectual and emotional mechanism—think tools—they realized the importance of using their brains and tools to collect information needed to go through life. Humans studied that aspect of human life in prior centuries, and with the arrival of the Enlightenment in the seventeenth century began a serious process of codifying various scientific processes of research that began emerging in the 1500s during the Renaissance in Western Europe. By the end of the twentieth century there were literally millions of academics, engineers, doctors, public officials, publishers, journalists and others, who knew that it was information—not just raw data—that was the ultimate prize people needed. It was the need for information why we had such large brains that daily consume 25% of our calories. It is time to restore information to its primacy as we contemplate our relationship to computers.

We are at a point when discussing computing, thinking computationally, or about the role and future of AI, that as a species we shape the conversations around information. Information is becoming central, the word itself is crucial in thinking about computing. It is why when biologists study the role of feedback and data processing in our brains we pay attention, even if their studies are of what mice and pigs think. We get it. As a species we have essentially voted that our AI has to be anthropomorphic, regardless of whether there are other forms of life or information processing out in space that we have yet to encounter. Philosophers and many computer scientists accept the possibility of alternative dimensions and realities that would make that possible. But for mere mortals trying to get to next weekend or to retirement, we are going all out for the anthropomorphic. So how AI is being designed is already decided. As brain scientists, neurologists and psychologists learn more about how we think and act, those findings are being ported over to AI design; we don't know how to create an alternative model of AI.

Besides, like our eye glasses and walking canes, we have always wanted computers to augment our personal capabilities. When we worry about AI becoming smarter than us, or be used for evil purposes to destroy the world in some horrible "mindless" AI-driven cyborg war filled with "smart" bombs, we are still articulating our concerns in anthropomorphic terms. We want to control AI, and for that purpose we have to focus on what information we get and use, and how computing speeds or slows the process. The problem, of course, is that unlike our own evolution over eons, we have pushed the technology so far so quickly that we now have to deal with its continuing evolution at a pace that our anthropomorphic forms have to keep up with, but that were designed to evolve more slowly. Welcome to the world of slippery slopes. If a scientist wants to engage in some developmental biology, what used to take months or years to accomplish can now be simulated in weeks. Want to change a mouse's genes to cause some altered behavior, you can work that out mathematically through simulation in days. It's the same as with studying millions of combinations of compounds to arrive at a medicine that has a high probability of working. There's that word again—*probability*. Biologists are now trying to design in or out of brains genes that help or hurt their owners. Designer babies are a realistic possibility, all of which suggests that bio-electronic hybrid brains can now be thought of as attainable someday.

Humans in mid-twenty-first century are going to have to spend a great deal of time understanding the moral, ethical, legal and social implications of a hybrid brain, one that has been altered or enhanced, just as our walking and vision have already. Until then, these issues will be of greater interest to the intellectually precocious and to those creating our brave new world. The case that computers can be programmed to be calmer and more impartial in a situation than a human is a weak argument for those at mid-century or for those closely involved with the issues today. These new issues or a less technical nature are coming and so the tough questions will have to be addressed, cutting straight to the heart of man-machine relations.

Think this is easy? One example from American life hints at the problem. Corporations in their modern forms came into existence in the last quarter of the nineteenth century, building on earlier variations that dated to the 1600s when Europeans formed companies in which people owned percentages of them that were used to build empires in Africa, Asia and most notably British India. During the twentieth century and even in our own time, American courts ruled that corporations (lawyers use the term "corporate personhood") were to be treated like individuals, endowed with rights such as humans enjoy (the law calls us "natural persons"), hence enjoying protections offered to humans by the US Constitution. Thus, corporations can sue and be sued, can be taxed, buy, own and sell property, and be subject to many of the same laws as humans. In 2010 the US Supreme Court reaffirmed the idea in what now is one of the most controversial rulings in modern times, Citizens United v. Federal Election Commission. Essentially, the justices ruled that corporations could spend money promoting political points of view and candidates under the protection of the First Amendment, just like real people. The key finding of this case is that rights to political expression are not dependent on the identity of the speaker, that is to say, individuals or groups (i.e., a corporation); all are allowed to express themselves. The howl was that a corporation could spend many millions of dollars flooding the Internet with messages and advertisements supporting its point of view, drowning out the voices of individuals with opposing perspectives. Many natural persons on the political left reacted in a perfectly selfish anthropomorphic way: They complained "not fair" because the constitution was written for and by people. No matter, the U.S. Supreme Court reaffirmed its decision in subsequent rulings. Political expenditures by a corporation were protected as part of free speech. End of discussion so said the anthropomorphic judges, or at least a majority of them.

So, can a future computer—a machine, not even a living creature—have similar rights? Since law is based on precedent you can imagine a human lawyer, or legal computer, standing before the bench arguing to some very uncomfortable judges who came of age in the mid-twenty-first century asking to extend the same rights to the great- great-great-digital grandson of the IBM PC or your Apple phone that the Supreme Court gave to IBM, Apple, Google, and Facebook earlier in the same century. That would surely trigger a discussion about the role of information and society the likes of which we had not experienced since at least the 1970s, with arguments for and against having different rules for people versus hybrids or just plain computers. One can hear the cyborgs screaming foul, complaining of racial profiling or some form of digital misogyny. Liberals would be pitted against conservatives; perhaps even causing riots and civil wars as the Old Order (humans) were constraining the rise of the New Order (machines). The philosophers and computer scientists would be able to claim that computers exhibited free will, as Harvard University's geneticist, George M. Church, argued they already did during the second decade of the twenty-first century. Free will is predicated on consciousness that even a 4 year old has; the discussion would turn on how anthropomorphic machines had become, at least until they could reshape the conversation for future devices that would turn on how AI they were in order to enjoy rights won earlier by anthropomorphically similar machines.

But on that path to such a future, what happens to mortals? We already know part of the answer. We start acting like a mindless computer. Already we make the right and left hand turns on the roads that our GPS system tell us to take, because we did not *a priori* develop a point of view on how we should go from point A to point B. We automatically click on a website whose privacy terms and conditions we agreed to without reading those, because on average it would take 18 min and a law degree to understand, when all you wanted to do was to order a book or toothpaste. We almost blindly do whatever we are told. In other words, we are beginning to act like those dumb computers we criticized in earlier chapters. If a computer continues to do what is already happening so extensively on social media—feed us more information of the kind we already like and agree with—how will we even know there are alternatives? Why would we even care to go through the effort of understanding those when we have AI to figure out what we want to know, how we want to handle information? We just outsource our thinking. What could go wrong? More paperclips than we need, more driving into dead end streets in small European villages, more fake news about how to treat medical problems or about whom to vote for?

Computers can only communicate with people through the medium of mathematics and the exchange of electronic impulses in combinations of pluses and minuses, positives and negatives, with inputs and outputs converted into text, voice messages, or paper documents. Talking to a machine or a machine doing so with us is an act of translation, and the computer has yet to understand values and emotions. However, mathematics—numbers—is a vehicle for communicating in both science and computing and so over the past half century we have forced ourselves to learn the language of mathematics across society to a greater extent than at any earlier time in history. Today's children are taught mathematics as if it were a language; it is essential in such fields as economics, sociology, *all* hard sciences and engineering, and in computer science. We can argue that the dominant circumstances posed by computing requires that we humans learn to communicate in terms this technology understands; Spanish, English, and Chinese are not good enough.

This raises an interesting question: Have humans been the hosts for parasites that are not just biological germs or atoms? Is an idea planted in our brains a form of parasite that finds we mortals good hosts, such as a religious belief or a national loyalty (patriotism)? Memes—information genes—can be seen as parasites penetrating our minds, and as such can be thought to behave and evolve the way DNA does over time. Is this simply a crude biological analogy, something that responsible sociologists, historians, and other scholars should dismiss out of hand as too simple, even inaccurate? Yet, historians and biologists have increasingly come to the conclusion that we can be and have been conquered by parasites. Their favorite current example is wheat.

Prior to humans consuming bread and other wheat-based food and drink, wheat was a haphazard, iffy proposition growing here and there around the world. But when it became attractive to people, it lead to the fundamental change we call the Agricultural Revolution, whereby people stopped roaming around as hunters, settled down, grew crops, ate well, thus had more babies, and became more dependent on wheat to eat than on the more various foods their ancestors enjoyed. The amount of wheat grown around the world exploded exponentially. If you are a member of the wheat species you would have to conclude that you had succeeded spectacularly in taking over big chunks of the world, training human beings to plant you (like bees help flowers to procreate too), eliminate your rivals for nutrients and water (weeds and other plants), and to cultivate you into more healthy forms. In short, wheat enslaved humans to do its bidding. Humans learned (or where taught) how to take care of wheat; it was a process of information accumulation by people. By the time of the French Revolution in 1789, it was pretty common for Europeans to consume 80% of their food through bread. Humans learned to take care of wheat and in exchange increased their regular supply of food. Remember that the next time you eat a sandwich. We are not immune to parasites and colonization. We are not only hosts to organic parasites. In the pages ahead, keep in mind humanity's experience with wheat as we muse about the role of computing.

You might argue this is a ridiculous scenario. Why? Because to believe it would mean we would have to accept the possibility that a group of wheat shafts met somewhere and consciously said, "Look, let's get these cavemen to take care of us. I know how we can make them do this." But biologists have accepted the notion that a species of animal or vegetation can evolve and become co-dependent and interact with other living creatures without having to have a conscious purpose the way we have that. In other words, there are intelligences and ways of communication that are not anthropomorphic. Bees work with plants, squirrels with trees, Monarch butterflies with milkweed, to cite examples. So why not people with wheat?

Ultimately we are brought back, then, to the primary feature of our ability as individuals and as a species to survive and thrive: to accept the centrality of information and so never to fully outsource that function. Like vision, we use our glasses to facilitate the reception of accurate incoming images, but then our brains still have the responsibility of converting those into information with which to take action.

Why Humans Cannot Soon Become Cyborgs

Prudent observers of humanity's use of computing reject attempts to have a serious discussion about half-human/half-computerized people, of bionic brains, of transplanting what is in a particular person's brain into another upon their impending death, of a robotic anthropomorphic (or not) new species sitting at the top of the intellectual and material food chain, because it seems like such a far-out possibility that could not be realized in the next couple of decades. But the topic cannot be swept away so easily, because computing already can do some things better than we mortals: remember, they (notice the pronoun instead of "these") process greater amounts of data and do it many times faster than we can. Furthermore, the topic always makes for fascinating reading and widely viewed movies. Because most prudent people may dismiss such ideas as fantasy, they may not understand some of the basic elements of this possibility and why it might be useful to at least consider current discourses about what for some thinkers might be the next—if not ulti-mate—innovation in the evolution of computing's relationship with humans, our world, and possibly other ones.

Let's begin by understanding the concept of singularity. If it seems vaguely familiar it is because in 2005 a computer inventor and commentator about digital matters, Ray Kurzweil, published a long book, *The Singularity Is Near,* which became a best seller. He predicted that by 2030 computer scientists will have been able to build a machine as smart as a human brain, meaning with the same number of neurons and equally important, the same number of connections among these. He suggested that this artificial brain would soon possess both greater intelligence and a consciousness of its own. Both features of this new device would continue to evolve independently of whatever we mortals wanted it to do. What their (machine intelligences') agendas and priorities would be and how they would want to treat humans was, of course, unpredictable, which is one of the reasons people nervously read his book. The moment such a computer becomes a reality is what he labeled the singularity. That is the moment such a device acquires consciousness and thereby initiates a new era in human history, when what comes next is unknown to humans.

We do not need to go through a technical discussion about how he arrived at the events unfolding after 2030; it is enough for our purpose to consider his hypothesis so that we can discuss its implications, because many computer scientists believe the technology will continue to become more intelligent in this century. Let them quibble over how fast and how much; it is enough to know that it is already begin-ning. Computer technology has a history of going through spurts of innovation fol-lowed by incremental improvements following such events. So, with AI possibly now going through a spurt, we can anticipate further discussion about the singularity.

Hold that thought of the singularity, as we turn to the notion of cyborgs. Most of us have learned about cyborgs from the movies. A cyborg is a person (or device) whose physical capabilities have been extended far beyond what we mortals have, such as by adding mechanical parts, including even additions to our brains. To be clearer, a cyborg—cybernetic organism—is both a biological person combined with mechanical body parts. This concept, along with the implied super powers that come with it, have splashed across screens around the world in such widely-viewed movies as *Cyborg* (1989), *Terminator Genisys* (2015), *Cyborg Nemesis* (2014), and 3 terminator movies released between 1984 and 2003 that made Arnold Schwarzenegger both rich and known around the world. Just in the last quarter of the twentieth century over 40 successful movies along these lines appeared, meaning that for over several decades people have been continuously exposed to sci-fi notions of cyborgs, and in the 2010s their children to Nintendo films. To be more accurate, sci-fi films involving cyborgs appeared all through the twentieth century; just that this occurred more frequently as we approached our time.

Before anyone smugly dismisses all of this as nonsense, pause for a moment to consider the possibility that we are becoming cyborgs already. Almost everyone knows someone who has had a knee replacement. People who have had their faces damaged in accidents have had plastic surgery to insert new chins and cheek bones made in a factory; and how about those dental implants? Prosthetic legs and arms with which the military have been equipped for over two centuries now look like something out of a recent cyborg film. Many such appendages also are connected to nerves. Today the variety of man-made implants is broad. They are used to deal with sensory and neurological problems, heart and orthopedic issues, to provide electrical impulses; add hearing aids and contraception implants to the list; even biologically developed organs are just beginning to be cultivated. One can sense that while a good *Terminator* movie is an exaggeration, it no is longer an implausible idea.

It is thus easy for the public to imagine the possibility of the singularity and cyborgs running around in the second half of our century creating whatever havoc or doing good deeds. AI experts have already started to contemplate the implications of their work so have opinions about the singularity. But faced with the realities of building such systems, they tend to be skeptical about how well, or how soon, all of this can happen. For one thing, some ask how long can we keep expanding the processing and data storage capacity of computers based on the base technologies used today? It remains an open question, just as brain experts studying 4-year old children begin to think perhaps you don't need as much dumb computing power to understand situations to make decisions. Neuroscientists believe the human brain is far more complex than even they thought in the late twentieth century. Now they believe computers would have a far greater set of hurdles to overcome to surpass the capabilities of the real one. So, first, current technology may not be able to scale up to do the work, and second, may not be smart enough to compete. But there is a third problem related to the second: that just having massive power—say all the computing of Amazon, Google, Facebook and of the U.S. Government working together—cannot translate into sophisticated enough computing, yet.

The problem lies as much with software not sufficiently advanced enough as it does just with the raw horsepower of computational machines. Software is still pretty primitive; just think about what you use on your PC or phone, not exactly the easiest to use are they? There is another problem: that software is not at a point where it can teach itself new things at the level needed for us to have cyborgs and the singularity, yet. Today they learn by adding data to their files and identifying patterns. That's essentially what they do, so far. In other words, they learn like people do, through more information and experience. To better us—to produce the singularity—they have to surpass humans, otherwise we might not let them "win," take over. Right now computers are being developed into more anthropomorphic forms. They have to get past that stage, and that is not going to happen any time soon. So far, they are assisting human thinking, just like eye glasses are human vision. So, because the technology has a ways to go, most think it will be a long time coming.

There are more philosophical issues with which to contend, too. Why would cyborgs and AI want to dominate their anthropomorphic creators? It raises the issues of wanting, of purpose. There is also why would AI transition from being gadgets, tools, or contraptions to some omnipotent God-like force in charge of everything? It is more realistic to think that humans in the next century or two would build cyborgs that can survive the cold and dark of living on other planets on our behalf. AI can gather data and test them against hypotheses—the scientific method of learning—but in the end, it only processes data one piece at a time, while the universe is both infinite, hence very big. We again bump into the problem of the 4-year old child's brain design versus that of current AI. Brain scientists continue to remind us that AI is far from displaying general intelligence. The often unsaid concern that AI could turn on humanity and do evil is thus less of an issue. The bigger one, borne out by prior history, is the threat of a human doing evil by using AI as a nefarious tool. If we can blow people up with nuclear bombs, as in 1945, that same species could do harm to fellow members using AI. We are left with the age-old issues raised by priests and prophets, politicians and pundits: How should humans behave toward each other, their planet, and their universe?

Biological Computers?

Our next concern is biological. On the way to the present, and while engineers were busying themselves inventing computers, biologists discovered their pre-existing computers, only they did not know it at the time. Today they do. If doctors can implant new knees in old legs, biologists "program" DNA (Deoxyribonucleic) to cure medical problems, what do they think about AI? Cyborg issues beg the question too: Will we someday have computers that are made out of living mass rather than metal, carbon, and silicon? The importance of DNA and computers to our discussion lies in the fact that the two behave in similar ways. Because they do, as a species we dare ask if someday will computers be made out of living tissue? While both biologists and computer scientists generally believe that is a long way off, we cannot be certain of that assumption, given the speed with which AI is now becoming a useful tool in biological research. In fact, a corner of that discipline even has its own name and academic subfield: Medical Informatics. For those concerned about the relationship of humans to computers, an elementary understanding of the concepts involved is useful.

DNA houses the essence of life. DNA is a molecule consisting of two polymer chains. Each chain has four types of residues, also called bases. The sequences of these chains are interconnected, so in nature DNA appears as a pair of tightly connected molecules—you have seen the pictures of these chains as twisting up and down as if vines shaped like a double helix. Within DNA are nucleotides, each of which has a piece of the molecule that interact with other strands of DNA. A gene is a sequence of these nucleotides inside of DNA. Buried in genes are the character-istics of a living organism, for example, the color of your eyes. Over the past several decades it became clear that if one could change part of a DNA molecule to produce a specific type of protein, then one could alter, say, the color of your yet-unborn children's eyes to brown or green. You could also fix a broken gene to reduce the risk of catching a disease linked to a gene or of developing a specific cancer.

The key ideas to keep in mind are that DNA not only contains information but also has the ability to transform in response to changing conditions. DNA reside in all living cells. DNA can repair itself, backup its collection of information, morph into new forms, embrace or discard genes, and be precise in its work. DNA is intel-ligent enough to recover from major catastrophes, using methods routinely used by computer operators to keep their machines working. These techniques include hav-ing redundant systems, ability to shut down malfunctioning DNA, and the capabil-ity of transferring parts to other DNA. DNA can store billions of pieces of data. One gram of DNA has the capability of storing as much data as we mortals can put on a trillion audio CDs. Millions of DNA can fit inside a tea spoon and process all their data simultaneously or, to use a computer term, with parallel processing, the current architecture humans use to design today's most advanced commercial computers. DNA processes data roughly 100 times faster than computers of the early 2000s. Computer wizards believe that silicon-based machines cannot get even close to such processing capabilities. And did I mention that the amount of energy DNA uses to do all of this work is a fraction of what our metal machines consume, or that DNA does not spew out toxic byproducts?

Both DNA and computers are worthy of comparison, with experts of one bor-rowing ideas and design points from the other. In the 1990s, software firms began to think of some of their work as similar to what DNA does. DNA is autonomous, while man-made computers are getting there; DNA is fully redundant, computers partially so; DNA can recover, computers only if the software has that capability written into it and if the electricity is still turned on; DNA adapts to changing condi-tions in its environment, not yet computers; the computer's capacity to store lots of information is constrained by the limits of our technology, not so DNA; both can replicate information, but computers have difficulty doing it well (i.e., garbage in means garbage out); and, of course, machines spew out heat, DNA massively less so. I think it is particularly useful to know that DNA computing can repair itself, something that our man-made computers cannot do. DNA has existed for millions of years without malfunctioning; we are delighted if our PCs don't hiccup for a week.

In a perfect world, computer scientists want to invent machines that work like DNA. It is enough for our discussion to acknowledge that they are doing research in that direction and that baby steps are being taken. It is possible today, as one exam-ple, to have molecules and computers communicate back and forth. That could be very exciting for prosthetic limbs and to connect man-made eyeballs to the nerve cells required to transmit images to the brain. So, we have entered a time of biologi-cal computing, but one that will stretch for decades before such innovations become part of the routine life of humans. But, experts are optimistic.

So, it appears we have a two-way set of developments underway. On the one hand, we can imagine companies like IBM, Microsoft, and hundreds of smaller ones building living computers in the decades ahead that make human uses of information technologies more useful than ever. I can imagine such devices being used to explore other planets and stars, to provide far better intelligence (AI) to even the most mundane human tools on earth. On the other hand, we can also imagine with just a limited jump in faith that medical researchers will continue down their successful path of reprogramming people's already existing computing capability—their genes—to address specific illnesses. That has already started and in the lifetime of most readers of this book will progress rapidly. Borrowing concepts from software programming and computer architecture, biologists are finding such perspectives useful in understanding how DNA works and can be leveraged.

Those two parallel and increasingly entwined developments is how we get to ideas about cyborgs not being so crazy. Arnold Schwarzenegger's cyborg's great grandchildren may have a future ahead of them. In the beginning, we can imagine as is happening now that body parts are replaced with new or enhanced ones, genetically implanted (or grown), such as organs and limbs. The sci-fi aficionados wax about how such transformations could lead to smarter brains and replications of whatever we have stored in them into other living creatures or devices. When that happens—and again I want to stress that those closest to the necessary research and development do not see this happening soon—as a species we will have to make some decisions about what and who we are and what we stand for. These are age-old questions raised by philosophers and clerics that will shape a new chapter in the relationship between mortals and computers, with the latter engaging in the debate.

We can imagine all kinds of things going well, or poorly. On the plus side, we cure diseases, upgrade the human species (everyone looks great) and we become better fit to deal with the emerging realization that the universe is a cold, unfeeling, chaotic reality in which our Earth is an exception waiting to atrophy in conformance with the Second Law of Thermodynamics ("Bad stuff happens"). As a species, as a living form, we want to survive and thrive and are willing to evolve to make that happen. We are cocky enough to think we can do this. We are possibly wise enough to understand why we should try.

Then there are risks posed by AI, too, to consider. What if we became cyborgs, where some AI supersedes in intelligence and authority flesh and blood mortals? Would these new forms want to transform our environment to better suit them? We biological beings need a tight range of temperatures and a certain concentration of oxygen in order to live. A cyborg as we think of them today—silicon-based—could care less about oxygen, because it needs electricity, not air, and why waste energy on keeping the planet Goldilocks warm enough for people? Go cold or hot, save energy either way. If we equip AI with our anthropomorphic values, that future being will optimize its activities and decisions to improve its efficiencies. A colder climate would thus be one option, one that would be consistent (i.e., compatible) with what AI would find existed the most in the universe. Humans are just too inefficient. So, a challenge for the human race would be to find ways to control and constrain the initiatives of such intelligent beings. If this all sounds silly, recall the earlier story about the paper clips. Experts in AI understand the need for building into their future creations controlling mechanisms to protect humans. Politicians and the rest of us still do not take these issues seriously enough, largely because we have no control over them and these environmental threats appear so far out of sight as outdistanced by more immediate concerns caused by climate change and CO2 emissions. AI experts would agree, because building neuro-networks is currently inadequate to make an AI brain capable of independent judgment, or able to make midcourse corrections without prior well-articulated rules of engagement.

What Does God Think About Computers?

All the developments described in this chapter leaves an additional issue to discuss important to billions of people: What this all means for their religious views. As computing becomes even further embedded in societies around the world, "first order" issues will undoubtedly be debated. One of the more obvious of these first order topics might include a renewed discussion about whether God exists. Or, for example, should humanity move to new concepts of God and body of religious beliefs that are less anthropomorphic? Second order issues are already being debated, such as the effects of computing on secularizing people in the most economically advanced societies, the effects of transcendence (whereby our bodies, minds, lives, even death overcome the clutches of our mortality), the love-hate relationship between religious thinkers on the one hand and technologists and scientists (hence computer developers) on the other, particularly in the Christian West. The high percentages of scientists, academics, and technologists who do not identify with a particular denomination adds to the tensions over religious beliefs. We live in an age where scientists are more highly regarded as concerns their ethics than priests and ministers in the West. Less agile IT users are reported by surveys around the world to be more attentive to religious behavior. Will that change or continue? The debate is on, and we will not resolve it here. However, the topic will undoubtedly play a role for the foreseeable future.

A little history from the West, where computers were invented and where the greatest amount of research on current and future forms are underway, can assist our discussion, even as China makes massive investments in IT R&D, especially in AI. In the West for over 1500 years Christian monks were some of the most innovative users of technologies (sometimes referred to as the "mechanical arts"), improving agricultural implements and fine-tuning farming practices, for example. They modified crops to improve wines and fruits, farm animals too. Benedictines and Franciscans come quickly to mind, but they were not alone. Images of their use of new devices appeared in illuminated manuscripts in the early Middle Ages. Productive work had become part of the way of life of these religious communities situated alongside their beliefs in labor as virtue mingled with contemplation and prayer. Theologians came to see use of technology as part of God's positive endowment to humanity.

In time scientific inquiry emerged out of these earlier preoccupations, involving the study of the human body, medicine, plants and animals, and the topic that resulted in a 500 year discourse within the Catholic Church: astronomy. In 1543 Nicolaus Copernicus described the Sun as situated at the center of the Universe, with Earth and all other planets circulating around it, thereby debunking the long standing Ptolemy thesis that the Earth was the center of the Universe. He shook up the astronomers' world and the Church (Popes and cardinals were, however, initially intrigued with his work). Historians credited his observations as a founding event in the emergence of the scientific method.

The Italian astronomer Galileo Galilei, who lived from 1564 to 1642, was next credited with being the father of observatory astronomy, having developed a telescope that allowed him and others to observe more precisely the movement of the stars and planets, including Earth's. He, too, argued that the Earth rotated around the Sun (known as a heliocentric solar system), which brought the wrath of the Catholic Church down on him, since it had maintained that the Earth was the center of God's universe. The debate continued, ultimately leading the Inquisition to find him dabbling in heresy in 1616, forcing him to recant in 1633 in a plea deal that led him to spend the waning years of his life in house arrest. During that last period of his life he wrote more in defense of his ideas. The Catholic Church banned his books. Long story short, the debate about his ideas extended into modern times within the Church long after the rest of the world had embraced his findings. In 1992 Pope John Paul II declared that theologians in Galileo's time were incorrect in their understanding of the planetary system. As late as 2008, scientists protested that the Church had yet to fully vindicate Galileo, hence continued to insult their work. For hundreds of years the optics remained bad for the Church, even though over time it had warmed to scientific methods and findings. To this day, many scientists in the West suspect the Catholic Church remains ensconced in some pre-scientific worldview.

However, humans have studied astronomy for many thousands of years all over the world, long before the establishment of Christianity, incorporating their findings into religious beliefs. Recall the Egyptians and their pyramids, Aztec, Mayan, and Inca Indian civilizations in Central and South America too, and myriad religions in Asia and Africa. Humans had long believed that gods superior to people lived above them in the stars, moons, planets, and in many cases also on Earth, as in volcanoes and mountains. The point is that humans developed religions all over the world that had several features: they linked to deities of superior power and intelligence to those of humans (often tied to the heavens), that obedience to such gods had to be a proactive conscious action taken by individuals and whole societies in order to gain the good will, hence support, of these gods in the daily lives of humans, and that they required repeated gestures to maintain such links. From those behaviors emerged basic beliefs, such as the existence of the Trinity of the Father, Son and Holy Spirit in the Catholic Church, even the simple notion in Christianity of obeying the Ten commandments, and the codification of these beliefs in what we can think of as "user manuals," such as the Koran, Bible, and catechisms. Religions all over the world carved user instructions on buildings and temples and painted murals, just as Christians installed stained glass windows to explain theological concepts and behaviors to illiterate parishioners.

How does all this entwine with computing? For religion to work, people have to make a conscious decision to accept its teachings and precepts as truth and practical, and to carry out its mandates, such as regularly praying, reading a holy book, and attending church services. Practicing religion is a purposeful intended act. It is an activity of an intelligent being informed by a set of operating principles (values). Priests are right in advocating that for religion to work you must believe, to have *faith* in its existence, regardless of what scientific evidence may or may not report.

Computers are another thing, as they have (yet) no consciousness, no belief system of their own. Some early proponents of AI viewed this new form of intelligence as having the potential to replace the human brain, what early AI advocate Marvin Minsky called our "meat machine." In the decades that followed, debates took place about the mystical qualities of AI that held out the possibility of a human's mind's content being preserved as a form of immortality, a form of transcendence, the singularity for example. Had religion become incompatible with science now? Were many basic beliefs within a religion now to be discarded as discredited mythologies, just as superstition and magic were with the establishment of science as a more useful way to collect information relevant to the needs of humans?

Such questions are asked at a time in modern human life when religion and science are widely viewed as occupying separate realms. As religious beliefs evolve, we see the two working out their differences as scientific findings and people's proactive desire for beliefs systems sort out. Ethics, faith, and scientific processes have co-mingled over the centuries. They continue to do so today. As AI is enhanced, the call for designing into such systems ethical guidelines has increased.

So too, has the call for AI to learn how to acquire such standards. There is a long-standing conversation on this point. It goes this way. If an automated train is hurling toward a crowd of people and cannot stop, but must choose to divert in such a way that it has to select who to run over, how does it make that choice? It is known as the Trolley Problem, in which five people are unable to leave a railroad track, because they are tied up. On a side track one person is tied up, and the trolley has the option of avoiding the five by diverting to this side track, thereby killing only one person. What is more ethical, to consciously decide to kill the one individual, or the five? Let's really complicate the classic description of the problem by adding current computing capability of knowing a great deal about all six people. The first five people are merely high school graduates, each with a criminal record, minorities of course, unmarried and all unemployed, while the single person is a professor at the University of Wisconsin on the verge of curing cancer and already talked about for a Nobel Prize for what he has already accomplished, is the father of five young children, and an active leader in several non-profit charitable organizations. Now what?

AI systems have and will continue to acquire the ability to choose alternative actions if defined in advance, less so if not, hence the relevance of the Trolley Problem, a known conundrum since first introduced to a class of students at the University of Wisconsin 1905 and still used to teach computer science students and to inform psychologists. Do you design in mandatory ethical standards? If so, whose and just as important what standards? We already know that expert systems of the 1980s packed with rules were not intelligent. Tell a machine to optimize the manufacture of paper clips and the world will be filled with more of those than it can handle. We are seeing these Trolley kinds of questions now spilling over into operations and public policy. In 2016 the German government published 20 rules that had to be embedded in autonomous vehicles in future years. Did it pick the right 20? Should it be 30, 40, or even 50? Who knows. Would a Jesuit priest from the 1760s or a Benedictine monk from the 1600s understand the dilemmas involved? Absolutely. Meanwhile, critics say the ethical problems posed by the trolley question are rigged to favor one point of view over another. Morality is in play and morality has always been entwined with religion. AI and religion have already engaged on the issue, bringing humans again to the debate about the future of computing. The outcome of the debate is absolutely unpredictable.

We are at a turning point in our essay. By now you should have had enough about human-machine relations. And I would agree. It is time to begin shifting to questions that bluntly answer questions such as "So What?" and "What do you want me to do about it?" If anything, the human species is a practical one, if terribly self-centered, viewing everything around them shamelessly through anthropomorphic bias, rudely and crudely discarding that which does not support its life, health, and safety. Fair enough fellow humans. We are a selfish lot. Perhaps cockroaches are too.

Chapter 7
Is It the End of Our World? How to Think About Implications and Challenges

We live in a world so seemingly filled with "fake news" and hype, and not just in politics but also very much, too, with technology, that it can be difficult to make sense of our growing and intimate dependency on information technologies. In the summer of 2019, responsible news outlets buzzed with reports that children were growing "horns" (bone spurs) on the backs of their necks from walking around looking at smartphones and tablets. Critics quickly pointed out that the data reported in the initial scientific paper was faulty, but the press ran with the story anyway, including the distinguished *Washington Post*. It reported in May that," kids are growing horns on their heads …. It's technology's fault." Crazy? Plausible? It seemed so if you already knew that the human species is capable of very rapid evolution. Feed a generation of children properly and they grow several inches taller than their parents, military medical records have proven that point. Play a ball game requiring use of your right arm and it becomes larger and stronger than the other one. Every outstanding soccer player has thick, strong thighs. We all have personal experience observing the evolution of our bodies in support of repetitive actions. So, notions of humans evolving so that their thumbs can text faster or their heads bend over so to read screens and walk at the same time seem plausible.

But what makes the story believable is not just our prior experience observing our bodies evolve, rather more pervasive the observation that it seems "everyone" is staring at tiny screens for many hours. Recall the surveys that pointed out parent's concerns about children's screen times, one that exists all over the world. The blunt reality is that the human race has already changed in response to its use of computers. That process has extended so far to so many people that we no longer are able to retreat to a pre-computerized life. Whether we like the technology or not, it is now a fixture of the human existence. The fact that this situation developed in less than a century is, of course, both interesting and, quite frankly, a bit unnerving. It is now the subject of growing study by economists, historians, sociologists, and educators. However, what is more relevant to appreciate are the effects of rates of adoption—what scholars call diffusion—about how we interact with computing, because we are still in the thick of a rapid and massive evolution in the technology and how

© Springer Nature Switzerland AG 2020
J. W. Cortada, *Living with Computers*,
https://doi.org/10.1007/978-3-030-34362-0_7

we mortals use it. That interaction of transforming technologies and our responses to it is the more important issue humans should understand. Such an appreciation can address myriad concerns evident all over the world: screen time for children as one manifestation, so too the role AI and other forms of automation will play in eliminating jobs (or old ways of working), the effects of fake but real looking news on our social and political institutions, social media's impact on our intrapersonal relations with family, friends and communities, and so forth.

It is time to take a deep breath, try to surmount the hype—since so much of what we read about computing's future is just that—and reflect on what might be going on. That has been the purpose of this book-length essay. In this chapter we look first at the role of forecasting, hype and evolution as concepts applied to how people discuss information technologies and the role played also by notions of revolution, revolutionary, and evolutions as they help provide context for the way we can think about computing. I advocate for looking at computing as an evolutionary process. I offer a way to think about its constant changes, what we get from the technology, and conclude with some personal observations about human-computing relations.

Forecasting, Hype, and Evolution

There is probably no greater example of hype in evidence since the 1960s than what people have said about the power, majesty, and future of computers. Thousands of books and millions of articles exaggerated and promoted information technologies of all kinds. It remains a growth industry with AI today, the singularity, crypto-currencies, Big Brother analytics, and Facebook watching our every tiny and big moves. We are informed as a matter of fact that robots and drones are about to take over everything; that 80 percent of all jobs will be automated within a mere few years, and so on and so forth. Because so much of this discourse is impossible to root in accurate forecasts (discussed later) it is just "blah, blah." And that is the problem: hype is not truthful enough. It is exaggeration, intended and unintended distribution of information, often simply dumb facts, falsehoods, and people having the really easy facility of being able to post their opinions without grounding them in the disciplined research long expected of experts. I have never seen a responsible magazine, journal, or newspaper able to avoid these problems, too, in my half-century of paying attention to what people say about computing. So we cannot just blame the easy access everyone has for expressing his or her opinions over the Internet. Where everyone seems to get in trouble is when they attempt to forecast what comes next. They invariably get the description wrong and always, always the timing, even those individuals who are knowledgeable about forecasting method-ologies where they deploy data and trend analyses and fancy mathematics; me too, guilty as charged. Add hubris to the cocktail and you end up with powerful techno-logical buzz. So, let's understand, first, a bit about the features of descriptions and timings in forecasting, because it is clear that people will continue to predict what is coming next. Then we can discuss some of the features of computing's evolution, what history teaches us, what the academics training future business and government officials have learned that can guide and inform you as you think about the future of computing.

As an historian, I know forecasting the future is a bad business; people just do not do that very well. In late spring 1914 nobody was forecasting the imminent start of the massive World War I, but by the end of the day on August 1st, barely 2 months later, it was on, and Europe went on to commit collective suicide. No serious technology commentator in the 1980s was predicting that over a billion people would be walking around holding smartphones in their hands barely 20 years later. But many of these folks did forecast that we would fly individual car-like airplanes by the end of the twentieth century, that we probably would have a colony on the Moon, and that at the same time, our cars would be solar powered. Forecasts that look out several years are fine, as they rely largely on extending trends already unfolding before us and that are nearly impossible to shut off without some dramatic natural catastrophe occurring: your salary next year will be roughly the same as this year's if you think you will have the same job; the odds of you buying a new car are predictable because the automotive industry knows how many millions of consumers tend to buy and what your economic profile reflects, and so forth. Forecasting—predicting—of that type—extending immediately existing trends—is pretty easy and accurate to do.

The exceptionalists are usually historians when they step in, because they know what happened just before World War I and World War II; they know what happens with unexpected events, such as a nuclear accident in Japan, a huge volcanic eruption, or yet another outbreak of Ebola in Central Africa. Chaotic, unpredictable events disrupt some of the best thought-out predictions. So, while I love to read forecasts, I know not to take them too seriously. Those "Top 10 Technologies to Watch for Next Year" are fun to read, and I confess to having written a few of those myself, but these should be taken with many grains of salt. Existential interventions disrupt all well intentioned views of the future. To paraphrase a bumper sticker that uses impolite language, "Stuff Happens." The grey heads of academia understand that this notion captures the essence of the ideas of existential threats and unintended consequences. The rest of us should too.

Humans desire to forecast the future so that they can increase their control over events. It is an arrogant aspiration encouraged by their enormous successes using scientific methods for understanding their world. But there are real problems involved. Fundamentally, forecasting is made difficult by reality being overwhelmingly chaotic—we know that thanks to scientific research since World War I. With so many factors at work, a tiny variation in something upsets the whole wagon. World War I started because one Bosnian Serb nationalist took it upon himself to shoot Archduke Franz Ferdinand of Austria and his wife, Sophie, bumping into them more by accident than by design because their driver made a wrong turn, turning down a street that the assassin happened to be walking down. That tiny turn of events resulted in war breaking out involving Great Britain, France, Germany, Austria, Russia, the United States and other nations, and that led to the deaths of some 37 million people, even more if we add in World War II, which historians consider an extension of the first one.

Since we know that chaos is more influential than order, scientists study chaos to understand how to order it. One type of chaos is absolutely immune to human forecasting, such as weather, but we can at least predict it out a few days, but not months or years. A second type of chaos is even worse, because predictions cause circumstances to change. For example, if a prestigious New York stock analyst predicted that the future price of wheat or oil was going to go up or down by a certain amount using a fabulous computerized modeling system what would happen? Stock markets would take that forecast seriously and immediately react by raising or lowering demand for such stocks, hence altering the price of these with the result that the original forecast could not, indeed would not, occur. A new forecast would simply reinforce the reactive process. Forecasts cause humans to respond to these to optimize or protect themselves from the otherwise inevitable result of the prediction. If this behavior were not so, why would you be interested in forecasts in the first place? You see this behavior everywhere in economics, warfare, and social planning. Hitler believed the forecasts coming in during late 1943 and early 1944 that the Allies were going to invade specific parts of France and so concentrated his forces at those points. The Allies purposefully mislead him with such forecasts and instead invaded France in the Normandy region with great success, a location Hitler had been led to believe would probably not be the invasion point. If Napoleon received a forecast predicting that the Austrians would mass their forces at a certain spot, he could be counted upon to alter his own battle plans to counter any advantages to which his enemy aspired; he did this all the time. The same happens in politics, where events are often unpredictable, such as any revolution of your choice, including France in 1789, Russia in 1917, the collapse of Communist Europe in 1989–1991, or the Arab Spring of 2011. Chaos and forecasting just do not mix well and the former, like all laws of nature, always outranks human thinking.

Making things even more complicated is how we forecast in alliance with scientific methods and computing, and how we speak of such things. Let's begin with the problem of hype, which is different from forecasting, but is entwined with it. Hype is the exaggerated promotion of an idea or point of view. Nissan makes the best sedan in the world. My grandmother's cookies are awesome. I met Mr. Wonderful last night. I am in love. I will make America Great Again. One well-meaning book reviewer actually wrote that I was "uniquely qualified" to write a volume I penned about how computers spread around the world. I loved the generous compliment, but others could have written the book too. Hype permeates all facets of our lives. Hype is not completely evil and misleading; it can call our attention to something we otherwise might not notice, such as grandmother's outstanding cookies or, in business, the need to start paying attention to a new technology or an emerging use: It is a good thing that you are reading this book, because otherwise computers would absolutely take over your life in short order! Book publishers' marketing departments love this kind of cat call. That is hype. It is also anthropomorphic catnip.

But it is purposeful too. In the early 2000s IBM hyped a new use of computing it called "Smarter Cities." IBM employees selling computers to governments had long noted that city officials were not as effective in using computers when compared to private sector industries. Yet, at the same time the political, economic, and social power of cities was expanding, so mayors needed to get on board with more effective uses of computing. Not only did city uses of computers represent a business opportunity for IBM, but the sales people also genuinely believed mayors needed to pay more attention to some of the contemporary management practices involving new uses of computers. IBM employees began to speak about cities being run with war rooms that conjured up images of NASA space launches out of Houston, Texas, from a command center filled with screens and rows of people wearing headsets staring at terminals. It was compelling and many mayors took notice; I know, because I interviewed over a dozen of them at the time.

They now wanted to fight crime like New York did (it was effective); Seattle sought to get people to use mass transit (done without need of computers); Stockholm and London aspired to optimize rush hour traffic through real-time road charges (a combination of policy and computerized road signs), and so forth. The poor mayor of Rio de Janeiro was facing the prospect of hosting a World Cup and the Olympics while living with a high crime rate. So, he wanted what New York had and correctly concluded that he needed it immediately. New York officials explained it had taken them some 20 years to develop their facility and all the crime prediction software and practices associated with it. At the time, IBM, nor anyone else, had a complete package of software and other systems that this or other mayors could plug in and use *that year*. Water management software was just being developed too, although hype made it sound like the Dutch had completed the job; New York how to fight crime and terror. Other cities struggled with how to handle traffic, address housing problems, street repairs, and provide education. All wanted or were using computers. These were functions mayors wanted help with and they believed computers could, indeed, should assist.

We mortals within IBM had to inform them that they could incrementally improve operations with computers, such as with deployment of analytics (statistics, modeling, etc.), pattern recognition, monitoring in real time traffic, crime, and consumption of water through the deployment of cameras and sensors. These were all piecemeal actions that incrementally increased a city's understanding of what was going on and to assist studying optional policies and practices. These were time proven methods for doing real work with computers. The hype had benefit in that it moved mayors to act sooner rather than later, although the Brazilian mayor had to realize he was not going to Star Wars his city in time for all the events.

Hype can be malicious, too. In the United States the tobacco industry hyped how doctors loved to smoke and thought cigarettes safe in the 1950s, until scientific evidence to the contrary led the American government to start warning the public about the dangers of cigarettes, beginning in the early 1960s. No matter, the industry's hype continued through advertising, so called "experts" contradicting the science, and with tobacco executives testifying before U.S. Congressional and regulatory bodies. It continues today with e-cigarettes, touting their safety and benefits, while reports began appearing in medical and highly respected news outlets about medical problems, including some of these devices exploding while being used, breaking bones and knocking out teeth. And teenagers experiencing a rash of lung infections. No matter, the hype continued.

My favorite examples of hypes are medical. They involve patent medicines from the 1700s to the present, most notoriously from the 1800s to the early 1900s. Snake oils, opium-based concoctions and other ingredients were promoted as cures for cancer, venereal diseases, "women's ailments," and other conditions. They were endorsed by "cured" sufferers, ministers, and famous celebrities. It got so bad in the United States that Congress established the Food and Drug Administration in 1906 to reign in all this hype. The British went through a terrible situation where their pharmaceutical industry hyped thalidomide in the late 1950s and early 1960s as a wonder drug, when it quickly became evident that it resulted in a higher than normal incidence of deformed babies. In 2019, American courts began to find pharmaceuticals guilty of over-promoting opioids, fining them billions of dollars for intentionally causing massive increases in dependencies and deaths due to the overuse of pain killers. Political behavior is so obvious an example of applied hype that we can move on to other concerns.

If hype is falsehood and exaggeration, why is it so prevalent in all manner of human activities, including so famously with computing? We all want—indeed need—to know what is coming next and when, so that we can optimize our decisions to our benefit and most effectively apply our resources. Businesses must understand future market requirements to begin investing for those; armies have to anticipate new war fighting strategies, weapons, and methods to prepare for those; individuals need to make decisions about where to buy, or to save funds for children's university education and for one's own retirement. The list is long and for each of these constituencies there is someone offering forecasts that are sincere or nonsensical; yet all involve some or a great deal of hype. But, the need to see the future is real and relevant. We need to understand our growing requirement to appreciate how computing will change in the next 3–10 years, while our curiosity about what will come along in the next three to ten decades is almost irresistible. How to begin taking action that optimizes both our use of the technology and control it for the betterment of ourselves and our species is normally a "must do."

To understand a technology's evolution, forecasters learned to take into consideration a number of activities and themes, since no company, industry, economy, or individual operates in a vacuum. These include the following dimensions: *political/ legal*, *economic*, *social/cultural*, and *technological*. Notice that trends in the evolution of technology is only one of four major categories to weigh. These four even have their own name—PEST. Even within the technological dimension there are many subcategories, as we saw with what went into Apple phones, each with its own features and rate of evolution. Futurists look for underlying "driving forces" that affect anticipated events, such as the current interest in how in industrialized economies' wealth has concentrated into the hands of a tiny percentage of the population, the "1 Percenters." Taking into account multiple facets—technological trends and the socio-political-economic contexts in which these unfold—has become a high art relied upon by companies, industries, and governments. They work best when anticipating developments in the short term (next 3–5 years baring another

9/11 or natural disaster), less so stretching out multiple decades. But it is not a perfect science, despite hype to the contrary. In the 1940s, when transistors were first developed, the wizards believed these would be used in hearing aids, instead the component became the foundation of the modern digital computer and for teenagers portable FM radios. So predictive methods have their limits.

What affects how we understand the evolving nature of information technologies? What have PEST-like methods taught us to pay attention to both as a species and as individuals? The list is lengthy, but also obvious:

- Pay attention to shifts in underlying circumstances in support of technologies, such as its cheerleaders and funding sources
- Observe the continuous, relentless innovations occurring in information technologies, such as (now) in AI
- Watch changes in regulatory practices and priorities, as occurring with respect to Facebook, Google, and Amazon on both sides of the Atlantic
- Do the same with how businesses are structured, as happens with Internet-based enterprises or in shifting localities of where work is done worldwide
- Track the rise of new competitors or sources of products and services, as happened when Kodak's camera business was overwhelmed by Japanese consumer product manufacturers in the 1990s
- Become familiar with changing demographics, as people get older in the Northern Hemisphere and younger populations expand in the Southern Hemisphere
- Monitor evolving geo-political realities, as democracies weaken and autocratic governments become stronger, or initiatives in generating innovations and R&D shift from the United States to China
- Become familiar with changing pricing and profits driven by political actions, such as occurred in the United States in the 2010s when the Trump Administration triggered rising tariffs around the world
- Understand the increased motivations to bring new products to market, such as to cure a newly identified disease or to exploit digital watch technologies to monitor our heart rates and medical conditions
- Track patent protections, which weakened in the twenty-first century, making it possible, for example, to have knock-off Apple products at a fraction of their original costs, notably smartphones
- Pay close attention to consumer demands, such as for less polluting computers, or digital products that consume less electricity, hence reducing their carbon footprint.

If you are reading this book, you are also probably reading newspapers, magazines and books, and visit Internet sites, so you are already being exposed to commentary about each of these considerations. View them as a mosaic as you read about how some particular technology is going to take over the world or revolutionize something.

At the risk of being too superficial, the effort is not complicated to understand. Thoughtful forecasters form a vision of the future in a conscious manner based on a consideration of these various types of information. They pay attention to things of specific interest, just as we might, for example, the options for cars in the months before we know we have to replace our current one. Remember, since the future is never static, we need to be prepared to change our views about a technology or social/economic/political reality. If a politically liberal administration is elected in your country, anticipate more regulatory activity with respect to carbon footprints; if a more conservative government comes into power, look to the largest companies to have a freer hand to pursue market dominance, and so forth. Baked into this last sentence were assumptions that have a direct bearing on technologies. They may not be the most accurate assumptions, but establish some that you feel you can act upon; societies, business people, experts, and government officials do so as a matter of course.

If you think changes in one or more of the list above is dominating and extensive, give it more weight, but make sure you understand the underlying drivers of that velocity. As many observers have noted the future, too, arrives at different speeds and unevenly around the world. Those realities suggest that we humans need to always ask questions like: By how much? How fast? Where? What do such trends mean for my work, my employer, my industry, and my personal life? My children? This calls for us to be like the children's story book character, Curious George. Thinking about the future releases some of the anxiety created by its ambiguity.

But note one other feature of better predicting practices: taking into consideration the variety of issues one must take into account. There rarely is one reason, one root cause, or one explanation that accurately explains something that has happened in the past or that will shape future events. All historians will tell you that; so will experienced economists and long-serving managers in the world of IT. If someone argues that smartphones will be cheaper next year because of competition—obviously correct—it is not the full explanation. For example, if a smartphone is sold in the European Union, to understand the future of pricing of these products, you cannot rely just on EU regulations; Taiwan (where the phones are made) might get invaded by China which considers the island part of the motherland, thus probably disrupting supplies of these products to the Europeans. That would upend everyone's expectations of smartphone prices for next year. So, if making pronouncements about the European mobile market, a forecaster would have to take into consideration Sino-Pacific politics. Add in what breakthroughs or problems American chip manufacturers could face and that would also affect European mobile phone prices. Impossible you say, since the Americans have improved computer chips without any break in that pattern for a half century? Well, rare earth elements needed for these come largely from China and as this book was being written, China and the United States were taking turns increasing tariffs on each other's products and already the Chinese had shut off the purchase of American agricultural products. It could also stop sales of rare earth minerals to anyone, including the Americans and Europeans. So, shun the simple explanation, connect the dots; too little happens in isolation from other events.

Terms in Turmoil: Revolutions, Revolutionary, and Evolutions

Armed with a perspective about the roles of hype and forecasting, we can next address the rate of evolution of information technologies and of human beings, because they are different, yet each affects the other. So, let's first clarify some terms most frequently used by forecasters. When Parisian workers in 1789 revolted against the king and queen and soon after chopped off their heads then formed a republic that was a *revolution*. When Russians deposed their Tsar in 1917 and in the course of the same year set up two governments, with the second the Communist one we remember from history, that was a revolution. Both shared two features in common: they represented a sharp break from the past and they occurred quickly. They were obvious to anybody.

Historians add another kind, where a process or practice transforms quickly, although not as fast as, say, a political change in government administration. Examples which historians point to are often technological, such as the conversion of manufacturing from steam to all electrical power between the 1890s and the 1920s or the replacement of horse carriages by Ford automobiles between the 1910s and the start of the 1930s. In both instances factories installed electric motors, while Americans replaced their horses and carriages with automobiles following World War I. In both cases life changed for everyone. Electricity and automobiles ushered in a combined economic and social revolution. We have even experienced one ourselves, the arrival of the Internet in the early 1990s, which people rapidly embraced across large swaths of the world as quickly as electricity and automobiles in just two decades. By the time we had our smartphones, Facebook accounts, and shopped online, our world had changed. As with political events, technological transformations are eventually recognized as representing a major break with the past; that they took 20 years is also conceded as a relatively short period of time.

All of this was made possible by the fundamental commitment of humankind to invest increasingly in scientific research, beginning some 500 years ago. It was becoming evident then—and over the course of the next several centuries—that scientific research resulted in significant benefits to society, such as improved health and the availability of products and tools of interest to people. It was also profitable, which proved important, because of the enormous cost of scientific research. For example, it costs billions of dollars to send a rocket to the Moon, often a billion dollars to develop a new medicine. But as a result of the word's economy becoming larger (richer) we could afford to fund revolution after revolution after revolution, with the result that the bulk of humanity became used to "breakthroughs," especially increasing in number since the early eighteenth century. We almost became numb to the process, forgetting that humanity was (is) experiencing a massive change in its quality of life when compared to its prior experience over the course of hundreds of thousands of years.

Then we have the word *revolutionary*. It is an adjective and so describes something transforming. If you were in Paris in 1789, you might have used it correctly to explain that the rebels were in the process of creating a New Order now that they had overthrown the monarchy. Someone in Moscow in 1917 could also reach the similar conclusion that the Old Order was now in the process of being overturned. In both instances to apply the word revolutionary properly would require that the individual deploying it would need to have a deep insight into the unfolding processes and events, additionally a sense of what the potential consequences would be that (a) represented a fundamental change from the past and (b) that would or was occurring certainly within a short period of time, usually in months or a few years. They would also have to recognize that not everything changes. The French would continue after their revolution to rely on bread for 80 percent of their nutrients, as before. Russians did not change their eating habits either until, as in France, bad crops and an even worse transportation system and farming disrupted by the political events made food scarce. It was always easier and more accurate to use the term revolutionary long after the consequences of prior events were better understood. It is always used in hyped-up text about anything, too.

Does this definition of revolutionary apply to our use of the Internet? Perhaps. Technologists, many social commenters, and pollsters would say absolutely yes; so too probably most people. They would cite the many hours each day people used social media, the percent of all their purchases made online, possibly medical and physiological changes in the human body (or at least eye sight fatigue) resulting from extensive "screen time." Economists would point to what percentage of a nation's Gross Domestic Product (GDP) went to pay for Internet access, Apple products, and the communications industry's growing revenue in recent years. Employees could pause and think about how much they used the Internet today to do their work as compared to the way they worked 20 or 30 years earlier. While I am sympathetic to those perspectives, be careful not to overstate the transformation underway attributed to the Internet. A personal example illustrates what I mean.

When I wrote books in the 1970s, I typed the text onto paper using a typewriter. I then put the whole manuscript and its illustrations in a box and shipped it off to my publisher. About a year later I would be holding a copy of my new book. Since the 1920s that was how it was done. In the 1980s, the PC came along with word processing software that made it possible to now use programs to write my books, making it easier to make changes, and so forth. In the 1990s, authors migrated away from early word processing software to Microsoft Word, which was then—and now—pretty straightforward to use. You get a blank screen and use a keyboard with the letters laid out exactly as had been done on a typewriter for over a century, and had at it. Publishers still wanted a paper copy of the manuscript; by the late 1990s they began to accept a CD or other electronic storage device for delivering a manuscript. Early email systems could not carry a big file, such as a book, so emailing had to wait until essentially the new century. So far, there is no Internet role for this story. Today, two decades into the current century, I can email my book manuscript to an editor, including photographs, charts, and graphs, or by accessing the publisher's website deposit the document into their book production system. What had changed from the 1970s through the 1980s was the speed with which a manuscript could be shipped off, and without paying postage. The Internet did not speed up or change this process.

The book you are reading is the same as those published in the 1970s (unless you are part of that 20 percent reading an online version) and the production process for designing and manufacturing the book had not transformed much. It still takes a publisher a long time to turn a manuscript into a book (between 6 and 9 months). You could conclude that the Internet was sufficiently transformative to declare it revolutionary, at least for book authors preparing and shipping manuscripts, or perhaps say, "well overall not so much."

But, we can also make the case that it was transformative. Research using the Internet changed, you know, the stuff that goes into writing a book. In the 1970s I had to go to various academic and government libraries scattered all over the country and in multiple countries to find the newspapers, documents, and books necessary to do research. I had to take notes or come in with a pocket full of coins to stuff a photocopier to print out copies of relevant materials. I spent hundreds of afternoons doing that between the 1960s and the early 2000s. Then, much of this kind of material became increasingly available on the Internet, if you knew where to find it. Today, I can sit at my desk and search newspapers, magazines, books, archival collections, university library catalogs worldwide, and "google" a topic to find more materials and, of course, consult the ever-improving Wikipedia on tens of millions of issues. In one afternoon using the Internet, I can collect as much (or more) information as might have taken months 20 years earlier. To me, research had been revolutionized. With that came consequences.

The change in research practices meant I had to "up my game," meaning be even more comprehensive in my research, because experts would expect me to do so (since they had too as well for the same reasons), and a broader audience for my writing would too. Today I rely on at least twice as much evidence for every sentence I write than I did as recently as 2000. So, the combination of greater access to more materials and the changed expectations imposed on me, and that I now expect of others, could reasonably be called revolutionary. To be sure, I could probably still get away with less homework, but the old ethics of scholarship, or what in business is called "completed staff work," had not evolved. The values and best practices readers have come to expect did not because of the arrival of the Internet, or earlier email; these change more slowly. So, revolutionary is a nebulous, albeit useful term. I think we are somewhere in the midst of this with respect to computing, much like riding a kayak traveling down a rapidly moving river with all kinds of surprises yet ahead of us.

Now we arrive at the nub of our conversation in this part of the chapter: *evolution.* Why is the term so important? We have all seen the cartoon of humankind's evolution from left to right with a gorilla-like creature dragging his knuckles on the ground evolving into a semi-upright creature, then into modern man walking fully upright. Some snarky versions show him holding a smartphone in his right hand. When looking at such images we accept that this was a long process, involving millions of years (in reality less), but we have discussed in this book technological, economic, and social events that took less than a century to occur. Hmm? What gives? There appears to be a number of problems here. On the one hand we have had a long process underway by which humans, indeed all living beings, change, yet on the other, people are doing so to information technologies almost on a monthly, or at least, yearly basis. At the same time these changes to the technology are incrementally affecting how we humans go about our lives, so not obviously in a *revolutionary* manner.

While we accept that our bodies change in an evolutionary manner we actually adopt new uses of technology in an evolutionary manner as well, as each innovation becomes available. It sneaks up on us. In the 1980s we lugged PCs into our offices and homes; by the end of the decade we had connected these to telephone lines to share emails and files; by the mid-1990s we carried smaller more portable versions on trips (laptops), while also acquiring digital cameras and figuring out how to transfer photographs to our laptops and PCs by the end of the century; doing the same after 2007 with smartphones; today across all our various digital devices and increasingly telling Alexa to do some of this work. But here is the lesson from history: We make these adaptions in how to do things incrementally with the result that we change forever how we do something so the next change we implement is based on the realities of what we had just done before. This has been true for all forms of computer usage since the beginning. Let's illustrate the process.

When, say, a manufacturing company collected information about what inventory it had and put it into its first computer in the 1950s, keypunch operators typed all this data onto cards that a couple of years later went directly from keyboard to magnetic tape; the older cards were thrown out, literally. Once in the computer, this data was looked at by software to determine when new supplies of specific items had to be ordered and that software updated records to confirm this had been done. Next with that going on management started asking their computers such questions as "How much inventory would I need if I increased production by 5 percent of one product instead of 10 percent of another?" "What would be the difference in cost?" "How long would it take to make the changes?" Then these managers might outsource to their suppliers responsibility to track the factory's computerized production schedule to insure they had enough supply of parts on hand, with each party using their computers to talk to each other. Today, an automotive manufacturing facility holds their suppliers responsible for knowing how much inventory the factory has, what the production plan is for that day, week, and month, and requires they have on the floor the right number of wheels, tires, transmissions, and other items. Going back to the old days of buying all the needed inventory and keeping track of it was now impossible.

Now here is the problem of perception. If you were the factory manager in the 1950s commenting to a reporter in the 1980s just before retiring on all the changes made, you would probably say, "We made a revolution." You would compare how your company tracked inventory on pieces of paper or ledgers, with the current system where you had automated production, used software that defined what parts you needed in inventory (or on the floor), and relied on your suppliers to stock the factory "just in time" to meet the demands of the workers assembling vehicles. That is a lot of change, so we can forgive the manager for saying he made a revolution. But, in fact, he implemented dozens of incremental changes over time, one building upon the other; each made possible by what had been done before. In no instance where a pre-existing use of computing or business practices is functioning do you see a complete wipeout of an old process by the implementation of a new one. When such radical changes are called for, management begins with a "green field" operation, literally building a brand new factory in a farmer's field designed to handle the new uses of computers, and they shut down or simply modify incrementally existing factories and software. The manufacture of Tesla cars might be an example, as was the construction of factories to make radically new types of computer chips. That is how things are done. What that automotive manager did was to incrementally and in an evolutionary way change how his factory handled inventory and production over many decades.

That approach, which my research confirmed was standard practice in over two dozen industries across over a half century made sense. First, the technology could only do so much in any given period of time, so management had to wait for IT innovations before trying something new. Second, most did not want to be the first to try something that had never been done before, because it was too risky technologically—such a change could shut down a factory, cause a lack of sufficient inventory, and destroy the career of the poor innovator. Third, most changes could only be paid for within the confines of someone's preexisting budget; getting extra money to do something new that had not been done before was often a hard sell to a decision maker. Personally, we faced all these same issues. You bought your first PC when you could afford it and after your friends told you that it worked and was easy-enough to install and operate. Your decision to buy a digital camera became easier once the cost mimicked that of a film camera and after you saw that others found it easier to operate than the prior technology. And you could afford it easier than, say, a new automobile. No fundamental shift in your personal budget was required.

Look at how you added new uses to your smartphone that you might have bought back in 2007 or 2008. At first you made phone calls, then took pictures and sent them to friends and family via email, then you began relying on these little computers to provide driving directions, then came literally millions of apps to help you order, do, play, and inform on all manner of subjects. You made an evolution, not a revolution. But today you might also say things like "Without my phone, I could not function, I could not do my job." "I am dead in the water without it." You probably would be right, so it feels like a revolution in how you lead your life when compared to, say, in 2008. So, we think about our relations with computing as revolutionary when in fact they were always evolutionary.

Thinking in an Evolutionary Way

As humans think about their relations with computing keeping in mind the evolutionary changes in our human-machine relations, soon to be human-AI/software relations, is a helpful way to understand how these technologies affect our lives. Thinking about waves of changes in an evolutionary manner dampens fears that the "machines will take over," the uncertainty and nervousness of the singularity. We mortals aspire to control our own destiny and to shape technologies at a speed with which we can appropriate them into our lives. That actually is how it happens, and has for centuries. This means that when we see marketing or techno-advocates telling us that something will "revolutionize" the way we live, how society functions or something is done, you are either confronting malicious and ignorant nonsense, or naiveté about how the world of technology works. You are being presented hype. Understanding evolution protects you from being taken in.

To be sure, there are spurts of innovation that bring about changes faster, but they are exceptions. Some of the obvious ones included invention of the computer card in the 1880s, development of mainframe computers as families of machines that could be upgraded and swapped out easily in the 1960s, development of PCs in the late 1970s and early 1980s, and smartphones in the 2000s. In each instance the spurt forward was the result of someone bringing together a collection of prior existing components or technologies into some new form, package, or product. The smartphone was made possible by Apple taking pre-existing technologies and integrating them together, such as telecommunications, digital photography, and GPS. In each example technologists had already been aware of the existence of the various pieces for ten or more years and had a pretty good idea of how they could, should, or would next be used incrementally. It then took someone to execute on these ideas: Herman Hollerith with his punch cards in the 1880s, IBM with its "family" of mainframes in the 1960s, Steve Jobs and his friends with desktop computing in the 1970s, and Jobs again with iPods, iPads, and smartphones in the 2000s. A similar tale could be told about software, although it was a more nuanced and complicated process. But you have Bill Gates in the 1970s looking for software to operate a computer and IBM finding programming languages and spread sheet software for its successful PCs in the early 1980s. IBM could go from a dead start to delivering a PC in 1 year by pulling together pre-existing components; Apple did the same with smartphone in almost the same amount of time.

After a spurt of innovation a long period starts in which incremental improvements are made to these devices and software. Microsoft has released well over a dozen versions of its operating system since the days of DOS of 1981 and many releases of its Word software; how many versions of Apple's phones have you seen since 2007? Then there were all those apps that kept being introduced to you almost on a monthly basis since roughly 2010 that show no signs of slowing. It is all evolutionary and incremental, shrink wrapped with hype and marketing. Hype is designed to cause you to take an action, to buy and install a new function, and then to make you so dependent on it that you cannot live without it. That is a problem we face today with social media. Going forward, we mortals need to understand hype and its limits. Keep in mind our earlier discussion about forecasting as you do this.

What Do We Want?

Is it sleep, sex, security, or food? The Agricultural Revolution began the process of making those available on a more regular basis than before, while the Scientific Revolution reinforced that these would be available in bulk, at least so far, and in consistent supply. But psychologists, psychiatrists, biologists and other scientists have been busy studying brain matters and are increasingly discovering that perhaps two things are in play as well. One we have already discussed and accepted—the desire to sustain our species at which we have been fabulously successful, going from a handful of millions of hunter-gatherers before wheat trained us to be farmers to today's nearly 8 billion people busily going about expanding to 9 billion. And what is the second one? It is happiness, and to achieve it, humans will use everything they have to get it, including drugs, alcoholic beverages, religion, love and even computers, if they can marshal that resource to do it.

Although modern scientific research on what makes people happy is in its infancy, what has been done so far reaffirms what priests and prophets have been saying for a long time: friendships, family, marriages and good health play profound roles in creating happiness, so too being content with what you have; greed makes us anxious and less happy. Managing expectations is key. Biologists now argue that chemical changes in the brain affect our mood, expectations, and so forth, a discussion we cannot focus on here. It is sufficient, however, to acknowledge that their argument is that our levels of satisfaction are not conditioned by ideas or society as much as by the interactions of chemicals, neurons, and the quality of our health. Biology reigns. Serotonin and dopamine are supposed to make you want to procreate, less so intellectual emotions about loving someone. In this scenario, biochemistry dominates and history is irrelevant. We are not at a point in our understanding of the biological influences to declare whether one view or the other, or a combination, is true. From a purely biological perspective, people are the result of evolution and not some pre-ordained divine construct. Life is a fact, not a meaning in such a worldview. Prior to the 1980s we could choose to fall in love with someone, to be happy, and to make babies as a willful act. Actually we still do, but the biologists are saying, "Not so fast with that thinking."

So what does all this have to do with computers? For one thing, if we individually believe that certain realities make us happy we will use the technology to assist in that pursuit. To a certain extent, for example, income makes us happy; too much income makes no difference. So we will use computers to get a decent paying job. Good health makes us happy, so we will use computers to make the medical profession even better than it is. We will build intelligent prosthetics so that we can use our minds—nerves—to instruct bionic arms and limbs to do our bidding. We already discussed how programming genes is now possible, but because we are in the early stages of using such capabilities we can expect that biologists and others will use computing to assist in further developments. I might even be able to have better eyesight and hearing before my life ends.

The next development already underway is the linkage of brain and human nerves to digital and analog devices that use some form of AI to facilitate the necessary interactions. Today we think of arms and legs, very soon eyesight and hearing, but right behind that almost sitting in the same bus with these will be artificial organs that will interact with our minds, hence our emotions, and possibly our consciousness. Maybe the biologists are right, it's about chemicals, molecules, and genes with a dash of electricity. Does this bring us back to the concept of brains being uploaded to the cloud or into other objects? If my brain is loaded into a drone, am I still a man? Do I have a soul? Or am I just another extension of an even larger quasi-living entity called Amazon delivering packages? Am I then still an organic living being or some inorganic object that is better able to live in a polluted atmosphere too hot or too cold for humans *sans* enough clean oxygen? What happens to religion, politics, or human warfare? That we even dare ask such questions beggars the issue for what our grandchildren will contend with as they sort through their relationships with computers. Philosophers will argue that they have been here before, but they would be wrong. The intimacy of computer and human goes from essentially an ignorant electrical machine to something far more complex than imagined as a serious consideration even in the last quarter of the twentieth century.

What Can We Get?

Are we at some crossroads? A central fact of humankind is that this species evolved, like all others, through trial and error, through mentally unconscious response to its physical realities. Decision making had been distributed down to the genes, to the DNA. Once the species acquired consciousness which it centralized in the brain, it was a short step to being purposeful in what it did, although to this day its evolution is largely a response to evolutionary practices pursued for over two million years. For the vast majority of that time it did not have the capability of intelligently redesigning itself. Today natural selection in many species are being altered by humans, such as with corn, cows, cats, dogs, horses, grapes, wheat, even mosquitoes and other insects to have the latter stop breeding. So it should be of no surprise that people anticipate redesigning themselves, or upgrading to newer models of pre-designed children by programming their eggs, sperm, and possibly the fetus during pregnancy. Who knows? They certainly have been trying to do so for a long time, from castration to drugs to alter sexuality, from nutrition to exercise, to imposing social castes that required, for example, that the son of a farmer would be one too, or dictating into what socio-economic classes one could marry. To think that artificial general intelligence will not be achieved and once achieved not be used flies in the face of historical experience and current reality. Given the option of moving from a rock to a hammer to pound something, you know the one humans took. So reading forecasts about the future of AI is more than fun, the thoughts of experts in the laboratories and cubicles saying grace over the future of AI should not be ignored, but, again, beware ill-formulated forecasting and even worse, dumb hubris.

What Do I Think

So far I have attempted to avoid injecting too much of my own biased, willful, even wishful thinking and naiveté into the mix of our conversation. As I stated in the Preface, I wanted to bring together consensus thinking about different aspects of human-computer relations that, I will admit, I thought should be linked together. But after staring at most of the issues we have discussed in this book for over 40 years, I have some personal thoughts.

First, as much as computing has evolved from mechanical relays in the 1930s to high-speed digital computers in the 1940s–1960s to today's miniaturized computers that fit inside bug-sized robotics and just about anywhere else, humans have barely begun to use this technology for much more than the accumulation, manipulation, and use of information to do tasks we have always performed. Consider this a long Phase One that began in the 1940s that has yet to complete. Yes, that use has changed a great deal of the daily affairs of people but since we have not seen the end of that people and forecasters will continue to predict mass unemployment as technology assumes more responsibility for mundane tasks and some dire changes as Big Brother is predicted to take over our choices in life and our civil liberties. However, as China learned with its Hong Kong riots in 2019, its extensive use of surveillance software and facial identification technologies did not stop two million people from pouring into the streets to protest proposed governmental policies not *valued* by local residents. If the Chinese government could have used extant AI to stop the protests, it probably would have. Instead, it had more protestors on Chinese streets than the French or Egyptians could ever muster. AI has its limits.

Second, all emerging technologies normally take 40–100 years to go from inception to practical use and AI is pretty much on track to repeat that pattern. As of 2020, I think of AI as being about 50 years in and pretty slow at that, since it is complicated by our anthropomorphic demand that it first mimic then exceed the capabilities of the human brain. In time it will do that, then probably morph into some form unanticipated today. The ancient ancestor that used a rock to crack a nut probably never envisioned a hunk of metal at the end of a stick we call a hammer, let alone the idea of specialized versions. The same will happen with AI. But what is important with AI is that in some form as yet still subject to much debate is that it may well evolve into a Phase Two in our relationship with computers. What experts are in agreement about, I included, is that it will be of central importance to the very nature of all that is specific to our current species. To be sure, everyone is all over the map on when that will happen, how we will know that it has, and what actually occurred. Everything at some point comes up for grabs: our consciousness, sexuality, religious beliefs, structures of our societies and nations, our physical forms, how we work, what we do, even who occupies and dominates our planet or planets.

Third, in the decades preceding that realistic eventuality, I see large institutions being the first to deploy this technology to their advantage, notably multinational corporations, national governments, and their allied organizations. Why? Because they can afford to create and operate such forms. We can anticipate that AI will evolve evolutionarily, not revolutionarily for the reasons I stated earlier, and they will own them to carry out existing aspirations until the technology teaches them about new thinking, new ways of doing things, and serves up new priorities. That will take a long time, but could track pretty much as earlier adoptions of technologies by humans. Once—and if—people are in the minority, it is anyone's guess and hype as to what happens next.

However, we have already given up some personal discretion in how we live in exchange for conveniences brought about by computers. It is a classic Faustian bargain: I will make you rich and famous in exchange for your soul. In literature, the Devil does not get to collect on the bargain, but in real life the technology often extracts a price from the entire human species, certainly from individuals. So far, the price has been cheap, but that may change in the next two or three decades as improvements in surveillance capabilities and medical innovations make the bargain almost, if not impossible, to decline. Most people choose to live over the other option. In all probability, the benefits to humans will continue to be compelling. Like parents all over the world, children's fixation with "screen time" is worrying, but for me, that behavior is an exemplar, a model of what the entire world could be like once the Internet and AI reach full strides. As long as the games are harmless and entertaining I don't worry about my grandchildren and their tablets so much, so long as they act very anthropomorphically too; by that I mean be able to interact with other human beings and animals face-to-face and function in the three dimensional real world, and run around to stay physically fit. Life's playground rules still apply, so too table manners, and the requirement that they share common values and socially acceptable ambitions.

I have long been an admirer of Stephen Wolfram, who is just one of those all-round smart inventors, technologists, and businessmen who think outside the box, but in a practical manner. We both subscribe to the notion that people think in terms of purpose and goals; computers yet do not, nor *consciously* most living creatures. It is because humans have goals and purposes that we can invent AI and computers. Wolfram dares to suggest that the big change in humanity will come when we have figured out how to be immortal, a condition that we are smart enough to dare somehow to achieve. It may not be in the simple paradigm of the Bible with people running around at the age of 150—that is coming soon enough—or in some ancient Greek mode where the Gods never die, but in some other form that our development of AI will inform. Wolfram is right, although I see immortality sometime beyond our current century, and certainly beyond my intellectual capabilities to conceptualize realistically, and—of course—it would be in some form that we cannot confidently conceive of today. I would love for my youngest grandchild to live long enough to have a sense of what that might mean, however, because one of the great pleasures of being a human is the happiness that comes from having a precocious intellect, a curiosity about how the world works.

In the meantime, as Wolfram suggests, AI will give us better options to choose from and, as we learned by using GPS driving directions, we will probably go along with its recommendations. We already have enough computers to equalize doing good and bad things and if we can keep that balance, the machines "won't take over." Leave that scenario to the movie makers and to those book publishers who have known for a long time that negatively frightful scenarios sell books. Along the way we will learn to think more mathematically, to write software code as a new form of literacy, and to interact neurologically with enhancements that back in the twentieth century we called computers. Jobs will change, old ones will disappear, and new ones will come along. Humans, if anything, are a flexible lot.

Let us tap into Wolfram for one final thought. He reminds us that we humans thought the universe rotated around Earth, the Copernican story. Today, we think everything rotates around us, supposedly because we are the most intelligent known beings. Phase Two may teach us that we are repeating the same mistake as before. We are after all the species that invented hubris.

This book has been short but a vast journey through a changing landscape for our species. The variety of issues encountered far exceeded what we normally engage with in most books. That vastness strikes at the centrality of human existence. It is becoming increasingly obvious that our interactions with computers stretches far beyond any set of tools, single narrow issues, or prior experiences that we have had outside our mortal bodies. Those relations range across all facets of the human and technological experience; I challenge anyone to seriously consider exceptions, I cannot find any of importance. While biologists document what we consist of and how we think, a growing number of we mortals are realizing that many aspects of our beliefs, behaviors, and physical realities are being influenced by computers. The Scientific Revolution may have brought us to this point and many of us believe it is a pinnacle of some sort, but I see it as yet another step in our species' evolution. If nuclear bombs, some pandemic, or a natural disaster don't kill us off, we mortals will live in an interestingly new and strange world where even the likes of the *Terminator*, Google, and Amazon will seem as old fashioned as we do today a cave-man's club.

This book began with the promise that we would tour quickly and lightly through a very big topic, how humanity and computers dealt with each other. But, as when we pack for trips we need to decide what to stuff into our backpacks, don't we need to do the same here? Scattered across many of the earlier chapters were suggestions about what to consider, such as our discussion about how to deal with hype and revolutions and evolutions, all ideas and practices that we should pack as we travel into our future relations with computing. The last chapter is a traveler's guide to what to bring along, should you decide that after reading this book that you want to continue on what is a never ending journey with computing. I have made my points, said my piece, so the last chapter is not required reading, but if I were your tour guide, I would still recommend travel light, have a plan, get ready to find life with computers still interesting, and hard to deal with.

Chapter 8
How to Live with Computers

Before you travel, you (hopefully) pause to think about what to pack for such a trip. You check the weather report, develop a plan for what you want to see and experience, book hotels, transportation and events, make appointments, and if on business, prepare presentations, reports and so forth, so that you hit the ground running and optimize your time and pleasures. If an experienced traveler, you pull out your suitcase and fill it with the minimal amount clothing appropriate for this trip. You set expectations for what you want to accomplish consistent with what makes you happy and productive. That means knowing your tastes, and in our case, who you are. This chapter is a traveler's perspective about how to keep up with the issues presented in this book; it is presented as a traveler's guide because no topic discussed before has come to an end, so, as long as you live you will be on a journey imposed upon you that you will share with in the evolution of the human race and computing. How might you make such a trip productive and interesting?

I answer this question by first addressing what it means to be human in an expanding world of computing, the anthropomorphic thing we talked about so much. I promise not to be esoteric or philosophical, this is a street level conversation that we have to have. Next, I describe tools you should travel with, you know, such things as passports and visas, but very different types than you might be imagining. Then, we need to know what to pack for the trip, clothing and so forth—all thinking-related items. You should be packing attitudes and ways of thinking. Finally, for when you get back home, what sources should you be consulting for years to come? The answer is more than just reading a bag of books, because too much is happening right now that you will want to keep up with for a very long time.

© Springer Nature Switzerland AG 2020
J. W. Cortada, *Living with Computers*,
https://doi.org/10.1007/978-3-030-34362-0_8

What It Means to Be Anthropomorphic

We have used the term anthropomorphic a great deal in this book for good reason, so perhaps we should begin with it. It means to be human, with an emphasis on the psychology of human behavior. I first heard the word used in a sophomore level college course in Biblical studies to differentiate people from God. But once exposed to it I saw it pop up in literature, fairy tales, and in computer science. It is one of those words that is physically fun to say, it rolls off the tongue so well and wow doesn't it sound so intellectual? But, it boils down to describing anything that has human qualities, so, for example, a future computer or cyborg could be described as anthropomorphic if it behaves likes a human. It does not have to look like one, although it made the replicants in *Blade Runner* a lot easier to conger up in Hollywood. However, human beings have an almost complete monopoly on the word. Video games play off this idea in their characters, such as in *Sonic the Hedgehog* (1991) and the Koopas turtles running around in the *Super Mario* games in the previous decade. If you say your dog is smiling because you see his teeth, that could be you saying your dog has an anthropomorphic feature, a bit of a stretch but the idea is pretty simple to grasp. We see anthropomorphic stuff all around us. Discussions about emotions, affection, conscious thinking, and behaviors similar to what humans display (i.e., playing, crying) are seen as anthropomorphic.

"My damn phone is mad at me, it won't let me make my call!" "GPS screwed up, now I am lost!" For a second, you would have granted your pile of plastic and metal anthropomorphic status. You would be wrong, of course, but it would reflect our arrogance in thinking things should be compared and contrasted with respect to how close to or different they are from humans. A great deal of what we have been talking about in this book has been precisely about those contrasts and comparisons as they shape how people think about and work with computing. At the risk of getting too much into the weeds of psychology, the idea of a living brand called humans has helped psychologists understand how human brains work, crucial as computer scientists continue to pursue AI, using our brains as a comparative benchmark for measuring progress. Currently, the thinking is what makes our brains function anthropomorphically is if they (a) store information about something from the past and recall it when dealing with an issue now, (b) strive to understand and deal with one's environment, and (c) use their minds to actively establish and nurture social connections. Children clearly display all three behaviors as fundamental ways to learn about their world, how to deal with friends, grownups and families, and the rest of us in how to deal with the politics of work, dating, and engagement with friends and neighbors. So, to a large extent, anthropomorphism is about how people behave.

As a reminder of a point made several times before, we humans are viewing the evolution and use of computing through an anthropomorphic lens. We are building these systems in our image and for our use. I am beginning to feel like a Christian theologian. But in all seriousness, would computers be different today if a non-anthropomorphic being had created these, such as another mammal?

An Alternative Definition of Being Human

That view of people worked well for thousands of years; priests and philosophers spent their entire careers discussing humans that way. We historians focused almost entirely on human history; you see very few histories of other living creatures written by Ph.D. historians. English professors only talk about humans, economists too. But, we are learning that there are other ways to define humanity and because these are affecting how computer scientists are thinking about AI and computing, and are taking actions based on differing perspectives about humanity, we cannot ignore them. The problem stems from the work of biologists over the past 50 years. We already discussed the DNA issue, but what are students of bacteria in your gut up to? In a phrase, they are expanding and changing the definition of what it means to be human. Instead of focusing on the software of humanity (how our brains work), they are focusing on our hardware (bodies). They have discovered that we are biological ecosystems and that we have outsourced a lot of who we are and what we do to other organisms.

Computer scientists and vendors of their inventions are paying increasing attention to what psychologists, brain scientists and biologists have to say about intelligence, cognitive functions, feedback loops, and how living creatures distribute the work of living within their bodies. We can expect such findings to shape their work, thus, the nature of future computing. That is why we need to pay attention to what biologists are up to, and it seems that many people are doing this already, not to inform themselves about future computing, but to improve their appreciation for the chemistry of cooking and to improve healthy eating and exercising. The leap from foodie to computing's developments appears to be a small one. Blame the raw milk aficionados for making such a big deal out of advocating that the live bacteria in unpasteurized milk was good for you. They have not won the day, yet, but they brought out of hiding an issue bubbling in biology labs in numerous universities, the growing realization that bacteria is good for us.

As a kid I grew up in places like Iraq and Egypt, where water quality was always a worry, where camel dung was widely present, a half century ago when washing your hands had not become the obsession that it is today. Turns out all that extra dirt in my life was sort of good for me, as it built up my immune system. Today, scientists report that children raised on farms with animals, a variety of poo poo, bugs, and other animals' smells and behaviors suffer less from some childhood ailments, notably allergies, asthma and autoimmune disease. The "hygiene thesis," as this idea is known, holds that children—and by extension grownups—need to be exposed to more bacteria than they have in the past. That is what happens when you drink unpasteurized milk, because bacteria in it does not get killed off.

So, humans are worlds of bacteria. They outnumber human cells in our bodies by a factor of ten. Then there is that water thing, we have a lot of water in us (60% of our body and 73% of our brains). Bacteria obviously wades in this water world too. It gets more interesting, because the majority of our DNA is microbial, yes resident in bacteria. It turns out that biologically we should think of ourselves as bacterial condos or cities, ecosystems filled with residents whose job it is to keep the community—you—alive and healthy and themselves too. Biologists have identified at least 500 species so far living in our bodies. From a microscopic perspective we are each bigger than any human city. The biologists are beginning to think that we humans should rethink our wars against dirt and disease, and begin to consider the benefits of bacteria. They are becoming sociologists with Ph.Ds in biology! Increasingly, people are acting like the mayors of their bodies. They are paying more attention to what is happening in their guts, diets, and more holistically perhaps than many Western doctors what is happening to them.

For bacteria to live and thrive, they have DNA, sensors and the ability to adapt to their immediate circumstances. Now imagine gazillions of them doing this 24 h a day in what amounts to a decentralized distributed processing environment where each microorganism is empowered to make decisions based on the data and insights they have gathered about their circumstances. Each is operating at their rate of speed, taking care of what is best for themselves and, you can anticipate, their environment. It turns out there are a huge variety of organisms mostly in our intestines, but all over our body too, all busy and they also include besides bacteria such other lovelies as fungi, viruses, protozoa and archaea, most living down there on the lower floors. To repeat, these tenants account for 90% of who you are and they own 99% of all that DNA that is so animating computer scientists. Clearly, we humans are going to have to rethink what it means to be anthropomorphic.

For one thing, as we try to make computers more anthropomorphic, will we have to think about incorporating our rapidly expanding knowledge about microorganisms in our bodies? What would that mean? Will we learn new ways to distribute information? Do our bodies have system wide communication networks that resemble the functionality of the Internet? Are these better than the one we have created outside our bodies? Are there operating principles and practices that we can apply to future computing? If so, what effect do those have on conscious behavior? We do not know the answers to these questions, but children born after roughly 2010 will probably have to deal with them when they become the future doctors, scientists, computer makers, business executives and public officials in mid-century. Their children entering classrooms in 2060 may first hear about the anthropomorphic in a biology or computer science class, not in Bible: Old Testament 201, which by then may no longer be taught if secularization continues expanding its popularity.

Tools of the Mind

Are we prepared to think about our current or future relations with computing? Like travelers we need to ask, do we have what we need to travel, like a passport? It comes quickly down to a form of digital literacy and our command of certain knowledge and thinking. We should begin by not assuming humans have this under control. A recent incident shook my confidence.

The leading organization of historians, the American Historical Association (AHA), has a spot on its website where members can raise issues, discuss problems, and seek advice. Almost all members have a Ph.D., or are close to completing one, so not uneducated slouches. Most of their issues deal with how to teach university students, both undergraduate and graduate, so folks between the ages of 17 and 27. In the summer of 2019, one historian wrote that she needed advice on how to teach them to read handwritten documents. She reported that many were having difficulty reading English cursive handwriting. Anyone of you reading this paragraph who are over the age of, say, 35 might be forgiven for doing a double take and rereading what I just wrote. What? Until the early years of our current century, children were patiently taught how to hold a pencil and then to write both block and cursive letters on lined paper to keep things even, then entire words with the letters flowing, connected to each other smoothly. We can forgive students who have difficulty reading cursive of eighteenth and nineteenth century writers as these were slightly different and like so many in the twentieth century, also just sloppy. But to have to teach the basics? Other professors wrote in recommending one textbook or another to get the job done.

In a study I recently conducted with a colleague, William Aspray, about how people used the Internet, we saw the same problem pop up, in this case, millions of people not understanding how to apply basic principles of scrutiny and critical thinking when staring at whatever was on their screen. People were having difficulty separating even the most outrageous fake news from even plausible actually true facts. These two stories are warnings not to assume that people have even the rudimentary skills needed to deal with computing issues. So, we should review some basics.

First, as in a real journey to a faraway place, we need a passport, used for centuries by governments to identify our real names, addresses, and nationality. For our quick journey through computing, our gateway—passport—into the themes of this book, are new forms of literacy and experience. You do not need to know how to read cursive, but you do need to be comfortable reading paper-based books and articles, others online, to be able to navigate websites and to differentiate those that are chuck full of nonsense, all in combination. One format of information is no longer good enough. You have to read articles and books, navigate the Internet and also your local public library, listen to presentations on YouTube and live talks at work or your nearby university.

Second, avoid the "echo chamber effect," in which you only read similar things, such as only what conservative websites say about American politics, since they repeat each other's facts and falsehoods (the political left does the same), or more specifically about our subject about how wonderful or horribly bad computers are and will be. Facebook is not run by evil people, but it is not always a well-managed company; Google does not only make materials available to you that it was paid to put in front of you, it also gives you the opportunity to see much more; the *New York Times* is not the only newspaper available online, both liberal and conservatives media are too, in fact, almost all of them are online. So, we need to seek out a spectrum of opinions and sources. Because computing today attracts as much passion and debate as happened in France in the 1970s and 1980s, pick and choose your sources but as an aware and discriminating student of the subject who is looking at a spectrum of opinions and facts.

As we do when traveling in a foreign land, good travel guides are essential. Both online and in paper forms, we only consult them when taking seriously the possibility of a trip, so do the same here. If interested deeply in traveling through the world of AI, know that computer scientists publish their books and articles through MIT Press, the IEEE Computer Society and the ACM, although tidbits of their work frequently appear in the Technology sections of leading newspapers and magazines all over the world. TED talks on the Internet are fascinating and reflect all manner of new thinking. Think of TED talks and newspaper articles about computing's evolution as intellectual eye candy, but cooked up with healthy ingredients. You should treat your mind to these; I try to listen to one 20 min TED talk every week, because I deserve it; you do too. At the age of 90 I will not want to regret not having listened to more interesting podcasts or eaten more ice cream. Besides covering every imaginable topic, this source contains a great deal about the issues we confronted in this book.

Now informed, we need to pack a bag for our journey into the future of computing and our relations to it and for that, of course, we should pack light. The most important item to put into our luggage is curiosity. Don't let the technology just come into your life one bit at a time, keep asking why is that happening? Why now? Try on new uses of computing to see if they fit you and is stylish and appropriate enough for informing you of what computing and humans are up to. Try new apps, discard old ones that no longer fit your lifestyle or are just dangerous or malicious; ditto for who has access to your Facebook world. If you worry about Big Brother watching you, put a piece of tape over the camera on your PC, don't invite Alexa into your house. Apple has already had to apologize to the public for its employees eavesdropping on conversations in our homes through Siri, (naughty, naughty!).

The most difficult item to pack into our travel kit, but so essential, is an attitude of openness to new ideas. The minute we start looking at a new use of computing or an emerging set of technologies, like cloud and AI, you run into the roadblock of ambiguity, if not actually into the unknown. Our initial reaction is to make a U-turn in our journey and find another path to take, another topic to consider, or we can simply cancel the trip. You could say, "let someone else worry about the implications of computing on my career, my children's education and job prospects and, as for grandchildren, that is too far in the future to contemplate. I can't do anything about it anyway." You would, of course, be wrong and in the process possibly do you and your family and friends some harm. You might not think through carefully enough how computers should be used in your company, so you become less competitive when a new Amazon comes out of nowhere. You could miss out on the opportunity to make sure your children learn skills they will need in the future.

My wife enrolled our two little grandsons in a summer programming course that ran for 1 week on how to write games. Not only did they love it, but are continuing to practice what they learned. Already, therefore, as 8 year and 10 year olds, if they had to write a grownup resume, they could put on it proficiency in Java, one of the most in demand programming languages today. But there are soft skills that they and others would need too, such as the ability to raise and explore the kinds of questions discussed in this book. So, you have to deal with ambiguity and that means being able to pull out of your bag an openness to new ideas.

This is not the place to run a tutorial on how to do that. However, it is time to observe that the best computer scientists and users of computing I have ever met did not obsess about the lack of clarity when starting on a project, because they had learned through prior experience that scope of a project, specific actions needed, and measures of results could be developed as they progressed. They were also a curious lot, eager to learn what happens when they take an action, because if something bad occurs, they were confident enough to be able to shut it down, to contain the problem. But like inventors who so frequently discover *by accident* a new phenomenon, they quickly notice the new development and ask the question, "Hmm? What does that mean?" That was how penicillin was invented.

In matters involving technologies there is another phenomenon familiar to experienced historians and leaders in business and government. It is the notion that if you keep looking at an issue, keep studying it, at some point your mind clicks and essentially tells you, "You got it. You got the big picture." There has been a lot of research around this phenomenon, involving many of the issues discussed in earlier chapters, such as pattern recognition. The "I got moment" is about connecting enough dots to get the "big picture" that then allows you to take in all manner of smaller pieces of information, because you now have context in which to file the new facts. AI scientists want to build that capability into future computers, but we mortals already have that capability.

War story. In the early 2000s I conducted research on how companies and government agencies in 18 American industries used computers, because I wanted to explain how that technology changed the nature of their work—and it changed it a great deal, as it turned out. I followed a routine in the way I studied industry after industry. First, I researched and read about how companies in an industry made money, what they sold, who were their competitors, what were their issues, and so forth. Then I explored how they used computers to address their problems and opportunities. It was a simple research strategy that worked. But because I had to look at some industries about which I knew absolutely nothing about, I had to start from zero. But because I knew a lot about some others, I came to the exercise intuitively knowing when I would know enough about a new industry to understand it at the level of detail needed for the project. So, I did not worry about not knowing how the life insurance business worked, or about farming. I did my reading, talked to people who spent their entire professional careers in these industries, and in every case, the day came when I woke up in the morning and thought," Ah, I got it, now I can move on to the computer side of the story." It happened every time and the feeling in my body and mind was the same. I was confident enough to move forward. I also noticed that with each industry about which I had to learn from nothing, it took me about the same amount of time to get comfortable with it—in my case 2 months for the industry piece, 1 month for how they used computers. The second part—

computer usage—came quickly because I had spent a decade building a large collection of files on how businesses used computers in these industries.

There have now been several hundred book-length histories of various aspects of computing written by professionally trained historians. They wrote for each other and for other historians of technology, so they are loaded with jargon and conversations about theories of innovation and diffusion, which is interesting to read if you are an historians or a scholar in a related field, less so for everyone else. Computer scientists do not read enough of these materials, and they should, because historians are learning what many non-specialists are about the evolution of computing. The conversation about ambiguity, for example, was a feature that dogged every machine developer from those inventing mechanical adding machines and calculators in the nineteenth century to analog devices in the 1930, to developers of the modern computer. Von Neumann was such a hit because he basically cut through the ambiguity to explain how the dots connected. Once done, everyone said "I got it." But it was so again with mainframes in the 1960s, PCs in the 1980s, and the Internet. Berners-Lee became a techno-rock star when he developed the World Wide Web, making it easier for billions of people to use the Internet, his achievement coming after the Internet had already been around for two decades. It is the story of how individual computer developers worked that is the essential story for computer developers to study.

With work underway on AI, learning from prior experiences is so valuable. Developers can learn to dampen hype, recognizing that hubris is setting expectations too high, too unrealistic. They already know to tinker and experiment, to try and then to tune, to model then build, to test and retest, to try out new software with people. That is the scientific way of working and it works. The historical case studies become encouraging stories about success, yet too few cases have been studied of failed projects. Historians need to conduct more research on why computing projects failed. Experienced IT managers will argue that many (perhaps most) come in late and over budget, regardless of complexity. They should know, they did this work. Successful projects overpower our understanding of failed ones. Adopters of new uses understand sources of failure: unrealistic expectations, ill-defined road maps of tasks to be undertaken in a prescribed order, sloppy scheduling, insufficient allocation of the right amounts of relevant resources, and poor measures of progress. In other words, failure is often correlated with lack of project discipline and insufficient space for dealing with ambiguities and surprises.

It is usually believed to be the core source of failure. But that belief is arrogant in that it assumes we know everything necessary to run a project. In the case of computers we are still learning about them, most notably now just starting with a new round of trying to create AI tools in anthropomorphic forms so that we can use these. I believe every adult reading this book will encounter more forms of AI than clumsy earlier versions. While there is much hype that all jobs will be changed or replaced by software, there is much to suggest that they will be affected, so part of your travel gear has to include a constant quizzing of what is happening to your profession, asking also what are the implications. Getting laid off is usually not the right answer, what will change that you must adapt to is closer to the correct response.

Behaving Like a Good Traveler in the Land of Computing

The most thoughtful students of human-computer relations share two practices we should emulate. The first I have hinted at: try out new forms of computing in both your private and professional lives. Be open to new possibilities as positive opportunities. Pull out of your bag a healthy dose of openness to new ideas and experiment, see if a new use fits you well and stylishly carries you into a new experience and success. That is what millions did before you when they bought their first PCs, digital cameras, and smartphones. Continue that practice or, if young enough, pick it up. It's like knowing how to write by hand, you have to be able to do it. It is one of the few ways you can learn at home and at work what technologies are "good" and "bad," to use good old fashion anthropomorphic thinking.

A second behavior involves a harder task: being an observer of your own ideas and behavior. This is difficult, because it is almost as if I am asking you to step outside your body and mind to observe what you do and think as if you were a third party. Philosophers think of this as self-reflection, religious leaders like the word contemplation. But the idea is ruthlessly blunt: see yourself for what you really are. In business, we think of this as both audits and reviews of one's job performance. When I retired from IBM, part of the reason for doing so was because I had reached an age when one should do that, of course, but also because I saw where the arc of the business was going and what it would sell in the future as taking more time to master than I had time to work. To put it in more elegant terms familiar to long-experienced high-tech folks, the "business was passing me by," and I was introspective enough to see that happening. I believe I could have continued working for a few more years, my manager told me so, and here nearly 8 years later he was still at IBM, so probably would have had my back for a long time. But, when you review your views, interests, and behavior as if a sympathetic but third party observer, you ask different questions, you reach different conclusions, you take different actions. Without all the changes in computing, I might not have thought to move on, but when I did, I enjoyed the benefits and, as it turned out, kept up with those events in the world of computing of greatest interest to me, not necessarily to IBM.

That approach to the history and future of computing and its relations to us and others mimics the behavior of observers of information technologies who also are its users. *Wired* magazine's founders and writers fit that mold, so they "get it" when writing about computing; so too earlier writers, such as James Martin at IBM who between the 1960s and 1990s published over 70 books about computing. Along the way you can gain interesting insights. I know, for example, that roughly 90% of PC and smartphone users do not want to be the first on their block to use a new form of computing, that they are nervous, even distrustful of it. Humans apply to their technology practices they use elsewhere. The mayor of Copenhagen was the first in the world to charge different tolls on his highways to control traffic, so higher rates during rush hour lower rates later in the day. He caught serious abuse from Swedish legislators and the public, until it became obvious he had come up with a great way to reduce automotive congestion. Then mayors all over the world began adopting his methods. He explained that no mayor wants to be first to do something, but the best want to be the second. We do the same thing with technology, so when you realize this, as an observer you can ask more realistic questions, for example, about how quickly and even how people will embrace new forms of computing. This is essential behavior because we do not always know how information technologies will evolve and even more important, how they will affect the human race, only that the wizards have a high level of confidence that it will. So, we must be on our best and smartest behavior in our journey to understanding these.

On Keeping Up

The issues discussed in this book are going to draw greater attention as time passes, so developing a way to keep up with its facts through responsible sources will become more important. Here I describe how I do it, recognizing that most readers will not be able, or willing, to devote as much time to the effort as I, but all of us should spend some on it for the rest of our lives.

Several mass media publications routinely cover computing for the non-specialist in a responsible manner. The *New York Times* is good for a thoughtful review of computing issues roughly once a month, often flagged on the first page or website. Both the *Financial Times* and even better, *Economist*, will once a quarter have a thoughtful detailed assessment of some trend in the use and evolution of a technology. For interesting, detailed, very pro-technology articles written well in an edgy style consult *Wired* magazine. For unbiased excellent surveys of how people use technologies and what they think about the, rely on the Pew Foundation's Internet & Technology reports, that appear about one per month and have for over 20 years, most focused on trends in the USA, but include global surveys too (https://www.pewinternet.org/). Finally, the IEEE Computer Society's flagship magazine, *Computer,* while it publishes articles written by computer scientists, these are drafted to appeal to many audiences and so many articles are approachable by economists, historians, business and government officials, and the rest of us.

In the past several years a number of well written books largely focused on artificial intelligence have appeared, all good reads too. I encourage you to read these and I anticipate others will soon appear. Reading one or two each year is sufficient to stay current. To jump right into AI and get a sense of what leading experts think, there is an excellent anthology of their thoughts, John Brockman (ed.), *Possible Minds: Twenty-Five Ways of Looking At AI* (New York: Penguin, 2019). For a short, tightly-written explanation of machine learning you cannot do much better than to read Ethem Alpaydin, *Machine Learning* (Cambridge, Mass.: MIT Press, 2016) and on computational thinking another short book by two reliable guides, Peter J. Denning and Matti Tedre, *Computational Thinking* (Cambridge, Mass.: MIT Press, 2019). Both appear in an MIT Press series called Essential Knowledge, which has many other interesting titles worth paying attention to and to which the press keeps adding titles. Since I mentioned Ray Kurzweil in the text, his book is *The Singularity Is Near* (New York: Penguin, 2006). A recent addition to the fine literature on mind vs. machine, consult Brian Christian and Tom Griffiths, *Algorithms to Live By: The Computer Science of Human Decisions* (New York: Henry Holt, 2016, and reprinted in 2017 in paperback). Another student of the mind, society, and technology and their interactions is Alex Pentland, who has written a book you should not overlook, *Social Physics: How Social Networks Can Make Us Smarter* (New York: Penguin, 2015).

For a brilliant yet readily approachable overview of the history of humans, a must read volume, see Yuval Noah Harari, *Sapiens: A Brief History of Humankind* (New York: HarperCollins, 2015). Since we discussed forecasting, see Nate Silver, *The Signal and the Noise: Why So Many Predictions Fail—But Some Don't* (New York: Penguin, 2012), and for an introduction to the role of social media and news in our life, a useful book by Hal Crawford, Andrew Hunter and Domagoj Filipovic, *All Your Friends Like This: How Social Networks Took Over News* (New York: HarperCollins, 2015). For a general history of how Americans used information with a lengthy chapter 10 on the role of the Internet, see James W. Cortada, *All the Facts: A History of Information in the United States Since 1870* (New York: Oxford University Press, 2016). Steven Pinker writes books about the brain and is not to be ignored. My favorites of his are *The Better Angels of Our Nature: Why Violence Has Declined* (New York: Penguin, 2012) and *Enlightenment Now: The Case for Reason, Science, Humanism, and Progress* (New York: Viking, 2018). Because humans are knowledge seekers, a treat is David Deutsch, *The Beginning of Infinity: Explanations That Transform the World* (New York: Viking, 2011) and an earlier, a bit more difficult read but useful in understanding how hard science has interacted with physics, computing and other related themes, *The Fabric of Reality: The Science of Parallel Universes and Its Implications* (New York: Penguin, 1998, but still in print).

I have written on the subject of this book for many decades and, as the technology changed and diffused, so too did my thinking. However, I recently studied how people respond and live with computing at work. For a short overview, see James W. Cortada, *Information and the Modern Corporation* (Cambridge, Mass.: MIT Press, 2011) and *The Essential Manager: How to Thrive in the Global Information Jungle* (Hoboken, NJ: John Wiley & Sons, 2015). In collaboration with another long-time student of information and technology, William Aspray, we explored how people were using the Internet to scrutinize facts, *From Urban Legends to Political Fact-Checking: Online Scrutiny in America, 1990–2015* (New York/Berlin: Springer Verlag, 2019).

If you want to understand the dark side, especially of social media, for an attack on these see Shoshana Zuboff, *The Age of Surveillance Capitalism: The Fight for a*

Human Future at the New Frontier of Power (New York: Public Affairs Press, 2019). For an economic and business oriented view of how computing is affecting work, I recommend reading Andrew McAfee and Erik Brynjolfsson, *Machine Platform Crowd: Harnessing Our Digital Future* (New York: W.W. Norton, 2017); they have been looking at this issue for over two decades. For a pro-technology view of future events, the popular IT commentator Kevin Kelly's recent book is a useful introduction, *The Inevitable: Understanding the 12 Technological Forces That Will Shape Our Future* (New York: Penguin, 2017).

Computers, like the weather, are always with us, there is no escape from either. Just as people of all ages are interested in weather reports and take actions based on what they learn, we should do the same regarding computing.

The inventors know what journals to read, what associations to belong to, and who to pay attention to as they go about the routines of their work. If you are not one of them, however, you might not have to read the sorts of materials listed above, but there are other steps than can easily be taken. For one thing, you can count on your industry's associations and their magazines to talk about changes in computing and potential effects on your job. They routinely survey people about their attitudes toward computing and on the effects it is having on them. These surveys are both interesting and informative; but be careful about the rest of the presentations, because they are often loaded with hype and unrealistic expectations. Take your own council on such matters and read with a critical eye. Government forecasts of future jobs and the growth in their demand are comparable in accuracy to the association surveys. However, more useful in many instances are those reports produced by government agencies describing the nature of future work, and those are worth paying attention to when peeking into the future.

For example, since the 1870s, the U.S. Department of Labor has produced a report, *Occupational Outlook Handbook,* that has described hundreds of jobs. These change as requirements for the job do, so you learn what are the current educational requirements to get into a profession, what skills one needs, what these people do, and how much they are paid. That is how we know, for example, that computer network architects, "design and build data communication networks, including local area networks (LANs), wide area networks (WANs), and Intranets. These networks range from small connections between two offices to next-generation networking capabilities such as a cloud infrastructure that serves multiple customers," that they are paid about $109,000, and they require a bachelor's degree in computer science. And so it goes for job after many hundreds of jobs. It is here where we learn that demand for such employees will grow by 6% between 2016 and 2026. We care about this particular position, because it tells us that use of Internet-based computing is going to continue to increase, which is a way we get to the suggestion that there will be increased use of AI by everyone. Descriptions of other ones can provide clues as to what could happen to your job. Similar reports are available from European and Japanese government agencies and are frequently reported on in the general media and industry magazines. They make for interesting reading and are useful within reason.

To sum up, the human race has engaged in a relationship with information and its technologies which is profound and permanent. That relationship shares many of the same characteristics as earlier ones, such as the adoption of fire for cooking, agriculture for steady food supplies, scientific methods to uncover useful information, and electricity to replace muscle energy. Each affected the physical shape of our bodies and the capabilities of our minds. Computing is just beginning to do that to us, and so, as I have argued, it is a complex subject worthy of the human race's greater attention in a more sophisticated manner across all sectors of society than it has so far received. Just as probably every boy and girl had to learn how to start a camp fire tens of thousands of years ago, our children and their parents all need to know how to use information technologies for their well-being. Doing that has to be a purposeful constant activity.

Index

© Springer Nature Switzerland AG 2020
J. W. Cortada, *Living with Computers*,
https://doi.org/10.1007/978-3-030-34362-0

Printed in the United States
By Bookmasters